ZIM'S

FOOLISH HISTORY OF ELMIRA

By Eugene Zimmerman

Foreword by Diane Janowski

Zim's Foolish History of Elmira
by Eugene Zimmerman, with foreward by Diane Janowski

For more information www.NewYorkHistoryReview.com

ISBN: 978-0-9838487-9-0

Printed in the United States of America.

This wonderful book was originally published in 1912.

For Archie

DRAWN FROM
DESCRIPTION
AND SWORN
STATEMENTS OF
ACQUAINTANCES.

Foreward

Eugene Zimmerman was born in Basel, Switzerland on May 26, 1862. The death of his mother in 1864 split the family, and in 1867, he emigrated with his father and brother to New Jersey. His artistic career launched when he apprenticed himself to sign painter William Brassinger, who shortly moved to Elmira, New York. Eugene earned little as a painter's apprentice, but gained valuable experience. Eugene lived with his employer's family at 303 South Main Street.

In 1880, he took a job at a rival sign firm in nearby Horseheads, New York. In his spare time, he copied the work of other cartoonists. The nearby *Syracuse Telegram* newspaper recognized his potential. Eugene took the name "Zim" as his professional name. The few drawings that Zim published in the *Telegram* made their way to the editors of the politically humorous *Puck* magazine. *Puck* quickly hired Zim in 1883. He left *Puck* for *Judge* in 1885. Editors at *Judge* appreciated Zim's ability to satirize both urban and rural life. In 1886, Zim married Mable Alice Beard of Horseheads. For a short time they resided in Brooklyn, but because both preferred the quiet rural life, came back to Horseheads. Zim commuted to New York twice a month for consultations with the *Judge* staff, but did most of his drawing in Horseheads.

Zim was the founder of the "Grotesque" school of caricature, and was the first caricaturist to incorporate exaggerated features not only in the faces of his subjects, but in the bodies as well. Zim is noted for his detail in his hands and feet.

By 1910 Zim began to publish books independently. His subjects included the art of caricature, humorous histories of Horseheads and Elmira, and tongue-in-cheek philosophies. From his home in Horseheads at 601 Pine Street, he established "Zim's Correspondence School of Cartooning, Comic Art, and Caricature."

During Zim's lifetime Horseheads' citizens were mostly unaware the fame of their resident cartoonist. He died on March 26, 1935 and is buried in Maple Grove Cemetery in Horseheads.

A Foolish History of Elmira lampooned local citizens and local history. There are passages and drawings in this book that may be offensive. Bear in mind that Zim wrote this book more than one hundred years ago in an area of New York State with no cultural diversity.

- Diane Janowski

BIG CHIEF "RED JACKET"

A monument erected by Elmira's first cigar store, to commemorate the advent of the cheap 5ct. cigar, and in honor of the fallen chieftain.

It has been proven to civilization that the cigar in question was the greatest menace of the two.

That looks to me a likely place.

WHEN YOU DEEM IT YOUR CHRISTIAN
DUTY TO KNOCK US PLEASE USE YOUR
KNUCKLES, LEST YOU MAR OUR ESCUTCH-
EON.

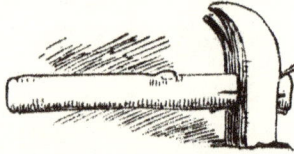

General Sullivan selecting the site for a monument to his
memory, on the spot that caused us so much thirst and anguish in later years.

"More than a hundred years ago, General Sullivan come throo here and cleaned out the injuns and after he got throo with 'em, they wasn't nuthin left but a pile o' horses he'ds. So our great grandfathers held a pow-wow and decided to call it Horseheads left went right to work and built a still and continued drinking corn whiskey where the injun left off. Don't know what'd a become of us if they'd found a pile of horse tails instead. Anyhow they didn't and that's why sich is the case."

After establishing Horseheads and driving a stake to indicate where Pritchard Hall was to be erected and that all future county conventions should prevail at that point, he (Sullivan) took a liberal chaw of John I. Nix, and ordered his troops to beat it for the Chemung River where his naval forces were concentrated. Having finished the great work of his life in establishing Horseheads, he ordered his gun boats and ox teams to proceed down the river (one by land, the other by water) as far as Wellsburg, N. Y., where a site was selected and contracts let for the erection (in future years) of a monument to commemorate his unwelcome visit to the Indians. Being quite familiar with the treacherous Chemung river and the

possibility of having his cherished hobby (the monument) washed down to Waverly on a June flood, he was particularly careful in selecting a site with some elevation to it, where now stands the pile of stone, which recalls to our mind one hot afternoon in 1879 when we attended the dedication exercises and paid five cents a glass for water to chase down the contents of our pocket flask. It would be well for future warriors who anticipate the building of monuments to their memory, to use this sad instance as an object lesson and advise in their anti mortem statement the erection of such in closer proximity to a licensed hotel.

Some men were born with a silver spoon in their mouth. In proportion to the size of some mouths a soup ladle would have been more appropriate.

Large solitaire diamond studs add to a soiled shirt bosom a most stunning effect.

'Tis folly to be wise in the presence of a dumb-waiter.

The absurdity of shining the rear of the shoe is fast passing out of vogue, only the toes should be thus treated.

Jones—Come on lets go down to the lake and skate awhile.

Smith—No I came out for a walk. I sit down enough when I am at home.

MORE REVOLUTIONARY DATA.

Since I began this foolish history many important facts have come to light, and papers to substantiate their genuineness.

Our respected townsman, collector of revolutionary data and relic hunter of renown, Ira Payne, has two rare documents in his collection which bear out (beyond question) the fact that Sullivan did perform his greatest act in this locality. One of the papers in question is a military order from General Washington to General Sullivan (or "Sully," as the Indians familiarly called him) and an acknowledgement of same by General Sullivan.

Both letters bear the ear-marks of revolutionary days; are besmeared with Indian gore, and executed in indelible ink by means of a modern typewriter. They read as follows:

"Headquarters,
Continental Army,
Newburgh, N. Y.

To

General Sullivan,
Commander of the Continental forces in the Southern-
Tier:

Advance posthaste, entire division, into the Chemung Valley. Plant our honored flag upon the most suitable spot for an Indian slaughter. Have dodgers printed announcing the approaching event and tack them on every available tree in the neighborhood. Have a care, I warn you, lest Dr. Cook or Commander Peary pluck your laurels. They are sneaking toward the north pole, but may lose their bearings purposely to do you dirt, by discovering Horseheads in advance of you. Ignore them. Please note also by the label upon this document that the Army has affiliated itself with the Labor Union, henceforth eight hours shall constitute a day's work.

If you have a willing and trustworthy deserter in your ranks detail him to open a (pigs ear) tavern, which is to be your base of operations until further notice.   G. W.

Encamped on Banks of the Chemung,
July 1st.

G. Washington,
Commander in Chief, Continental Army,
Newburgh, N. Y.

Dear General:—

Your order dated Christmas morning received this first day of July. You can reckon on obedience as my troops have become despondent through lack of exercise.

„They have worn out five croquet sets and ten decks of cards during the lull in hostilities and many of my most earnest deserters have married into the foremost families of Redskins.

As it is now past six P. M., and the eight hour Union Labor ban is over me I shall defer my inventory of the remaining enthusiasm in my ranks till sunrise.

In the course of a week I expect to be able to consign to you by way of special canal boat one thousand adult Indian scalps and ten tons of arrow heads. Kindly look up market quotations on Indian relics and advise me.

                           Adieux,

P. S.—Presuming this acknowledgement will reach you about December 25th, I will add "A Merry Christmas to you and your staff."   SULLY.

General Sullivan dictating an acknowledgment of his error to his portable military secretary.

When General Sullivan assumed command of the army, he was fully aware of his ignorance of the country he was about to invade. He had, so far, heard nothing of the wonderful celery and lettuce gardens of Horseheads; the asparagus and garlic beds of Pine Valley, nor the **Simon Pure Havana** tobacco fields of Big Flats. Had the general troubled himself to inquire into the locality's conditions before advancing hither, he might have saved the original thirteen states many hundreds of dollars, which were ruthlessly and uselessly squandered on inferior canned "delicatessen" upon which the army, much against its wishes, was obliged to subsist. We forgive the general, however, for his lack of foresight, for as soon as his attention was directed to his shortcomings and he discovered his error, he at once dictated to his lady stenographer an acknowledgment of same, thus avoiding a court martial or military inquiry and possible degradation or exile.

Forthwith he ordered his army placed on double rations, not to conceal his mistake, but to rid his commissary department of the fifty-seven varieties of canned goods as hastily as possible.

There being as yet no engagements booked with the Indians—(it would have been a grave breach of military decorum to disturb them without first serving two weeks' notice to vacate)—the general detailed one-half of his idle command to explore the rifts for dobson and tonies and set the other half to catching bass. From that moment his entire command lived as only good soldiers should —on the best that land and river afforded. In his annual report to General Washington, Sullivan omitted these facts; consequently they have not found their way into history.

OUCH!

P. S.—Some of my readers may feel disposed to inquire where they got all their fish hooks and lines. To these I would answer that, hooks and lines were part of each soldier's equipment and just as essential as russett polish and Florida water and shaving sticks are to the soldiers of our time.

   While advancing up the river road just opposite the Fair Grounds, Gen. Sullivan's supply train
was surprised and attacked by a band of hostiles.
The commissary officer ordered much of the stuff
eaten there and then, and otherwise destroyed,
and a quantity of cold storage eggs were sunk
into an obscure well which after a decade or two
began to belch forth water of wonderful aroma.
This water was carefully analyzed by a local
chemist who pronounced it the finest natural sul-
phur spring of the age. Presently a sanatarium
was erected over the spot and christened "Baden-
Baden" and for a quarter of a century it served
to eradicate rheumatism and gout from the valley.
The place went down in history (like its neighbors, the old brewery and the pest house) some
time in the nineteenth century.

   Pea soup and other remnants of a sumptous repast, carelessly slopped down the front of a fancy vest, gives one an
air of negligee and will attract much attention.

SULLIVAN'S CANNON.

It is stated upon good and reliable authority
(now deceased) that General Sullivan, to keep the
same beyond the reach of the enemy, buried in
the neighborhood of Horseheads, a valuable brass
cannon. Every spring, when the top soil is awak-
ened from its winter's slumber, by the rusty
plowshare, one may see many devout searchers
with divining rods, in quest of the modern Capt.
Kidd treasure. Outsiders wishing to participate
in the search can do so by registering their proper names (or aliases) with the village clerk and
securing a gun license to defend their right and
title in case of discovery.

RORICKS GLEN

Roricks Glen came by its name honorably, for
and in consideration of a few shillings. The Glen
was originally an Indian abode, much like the
rest of Chemung County. It was the intention of
its original Indian owner to hold the property for
a higher bid, having been put wise to the fact that
before many years the Elmira Water, Light and
Railroad Co. would extend its lines there and
build a whirly-gig affair in the neighborhood,

which would greatly enhance the value of said property, but his (jug) spirits were discouragingly low and he had been without tobacco for more than a fortnight, and smoking dead grass and autumn leaves was anything but desirable to a full fledged Indian. To add still further to his misery his season's crop of arrow-heads turned out a flat failure, so in despair he sold to one Rorick the acres of his forefathers and foremothers, for a mere song, yet it is said by those who knew Rorick well, that he was a "bum" singer. The deal was consummated nevertheless, with due Indian pomp.

The Glen is now one of the popular resorts of the State, and ranks next to the Reformatory as a drawing feature. However, the patronage of the Glen is only local, and uncertain on account of climatic changes. That of the Reformatory is far reaching and reliable the year 'round.

Solemn and impressive ceremony attending the original purchase of Roricks Glen from the Red man.

Why do women persist in writing secrets upon postal cards, and adding "but for heaven's sake don't say I told you-"

Pension Agent—So you were only a common private all through the war, hey?

O'Brien—Faith, yez be wrong, sor, I got to be a desertor before it was half over wid.

"BOHEMIA"

That delightful spot up the Chemung River was once the natural stamping ground of rattle-snakes and the lazy reds. One fine spring day when the crows were seeking new mates and gathering drift wood with which to build their nests for the ensuing year, and the river was slowly wending its way down stream as usual, a pale face, of business and pleasure instincts, was observed chugging his way, in a borrowed automobile, along the narrow Indian trail. He wore about his person an insignia which at once commanded respect, a red shirt and white helmet which lent or even gave to his stubbiness an awe inspiring effect. Evidently he was a member (of no mean degree) of the "Exempts," a dauntless tribe of pale faces much sought at parades and respected by the world at large, and justly applauded.

There were no doubts in the minds of the redskins but that this formidable looking person of the red shirt was a man of note, for in the transaction he offered one of ninety days' duration, bearing legal interest and payable at the Second National Bank every quarter of each year of its existence.

Indians, bear you in mind, were hard folks to deal with, especially when it involved paper securities or watered stocks. They sternly demanded equivalent in something substantial, some-

thing that really existed. Thus the clever Yankee
of the red shirt offered in the trade one second
hand water front range and three lengths of stove
pipe with elbows to fit and match, and thus you
have the truthless and unreliable story of the purchase of Bohemia. It was a "Happy Thought"
indeed, for ever since its acquisition many tribes
have held their pow-wows upon that spot and are
willing and able to attest to the fact that the foot
hills along the narrows were too good for the common and lazy reds.

Trousers with baggy knees should dangle from one sus-
pender only, and cotton socks (of a cheap grade) should
overhang the shoe tops with laces untied and fluttering leisurely in the atmosphere. This makes a very smart com-
bination for the hot weather.

A man's poverty is often hidden beneath his coat tails.
It would be rather embarrassing to raise a stranger's coat
tails to learn his financial standing, so we let Dunn and
Bradstreet make the necessary discoveries for us.

ELMIRA

Entering the City of Elmira from the East by way of the good old reliable Erie the eye is treated to a picture of modern Venice, (if one will permit his imagination to wander so far away). Overhanging Chemung's high banks may be seen the rugged rears of many four story villas of solid brick and mortar, beautifully festooned in bewildering color schemes of weekly washings and ash cans of less brilliant tints—a bit of whitewash and dishwater carelessly slopped here and there upon the vineless clad walls that rise so majestically toward the better air above, their foundations licked by the lazy waters of that beautiful stream.

Here may be seen also the ancient gondola of the city scavenger, with its cheerful faced and mellow, Venetian voiced, gondolier raking from its shallow depths the pearly oyster shells and other stray "bric-a-brac" for which that waterway is so justly noted, the whole blending into a scene of indescribable splendor. A picture long to be remembered, or not easily to be forgotten.

The American people worry a heap. They worry about everything in fact, and when they have nothing further to worry about, they worry about that.

WATER STREET

Water street, which is the money center and shopping district, is built dangerously close to the river's edge, yet agreeably so for those who regard water in the light of a necessary adulterant or a desirable blender of spirits fermenti. It is built so close to the Chemung's banks as to be deemed an encroachment on the river's rights, thus the river finds it necessary every spring to utilize Water Street as a temporary waterway. It is also compelled to store away many gallons of its aqua in cellars along the line—the accommodating merchants, recognizing the river's right of way, courteously remove their wares without hesitation from their cellars to higher quarters to make room for this most formidable element.

The high water mark is set at the Lyceum Theatre. Under the laws of gravity the river is not allowed to proceed above that point. It is no uncommon sight to behold theatre parties arriving in flat bottom boats when these conditions prevail and numerous private skiffs tied to hitching posts for those who have business to transact, between the acts, in nearby cafes.

Mercy how the purse strings of some folks do squeak when they are asked to help along a good cause.

The fame of Elmira has reached far into the interior of Hoboken. A ferry boat plying between two states at that point, bears its proud name and has proven a welcome sign to more than one homecoming Elmiran after one of those Chemung Society annual dinners, when one feels the need of cracked ice and conjugal sympathy.

It gives one much the same feeling as the American tourist experiences when he beholds in a foreign land his beloved Stars and Stripes, only more so.

ANSWERS FOR THE ANXIOUS.

Dear Sir:—

If a spiritual adviser enters a sick room where he finds his family physician in attendance and after greeting the doctor turns to the patient and in solemn voice implores him to prepare for the better life beyond, would you consider it a direct reflection upon the good and kind doctor?
Dear Madam:—

Give us the size of the sick room, the color of eyes and hair of the patient and the name of the doctor (never mind the parson) else we refuse to answer.

Elmira, as a peaceable city, has few equals. Under the watchful eye of Chief Cassada and his able and obliging staff of club swingers, peace and quiet reigns supreme. It is seldom that it becomes absolutely necessary to wake up the cop during his hours of somnambulism—and as for courtesy (If you will permit me to express myself in the vernacular of good society), he's ever there with the goods, and so kind and gentle hearted are these men of the Elmira force that I have seen them while on duty, amusing youngsters with simple games to divert their tender minds from mischief.

Those who follow the ponies for profit had better watch our friend Updike of Horseheads.

This gentleman has no use for favorites, but invests in rank outsiders. He takes only one kind of bet, that is that his horse will come in head first. So far he has never lost a bet.

The Lord may love a cheerful giver, but there are many who are willing to sacrifice that distinction.

"MUGGED"

CHIEF FRANK CASSADA

GEN'L J. SULLIVAN

Representing ye House of ye
WASHINGTON AND STAFFE

Newburge, N. Yorke.

CONDUCTING YE BUSYNESS IN YE

Indyan Hydes, Pelts, Scalps,
and Relycks.

Facsimile of Sullivan's visiting card which he used on
state occasions—when calling upon Indian Chiefs to make
terms for the purchase of scalps in advance of a battle.

Schornstheimer's Corners is a famous place of amusement. It is the Fourth of July meeting place of the Senators, a temperance(?)body. It is also one of the few places in Elmira where "Fromage" is allowed to roam around unmuzzled at that season of the year. The place is handy to the car lines and those overwhelmed by the excitement of the day may find convenient places of repose in and adjacent to the park.

TO AVOID MOSQUITO BITES.
Take one pint of coal tar, rub it thoroughly into the pores of the skin and hair and sprinkle generously with live geese feathers. The tar will repel attack, but if the pests be too persistent the feathers will tickle him to death.

This book is on sale at all aerial and submarine news stands.

Holes in the heels of socks worn with low cut shoes are considered the proper thing in good society.

In the early history of Elmira, the Chemung
River behaved very badly, so that it was necessary
to dam it some. It was dammed in every language known to Elmirans, and in many cases it
did this unruly stream but little good. When the
Chase Hibbard mill was built it got so thoroughly
dammed from shore to shore, that she never fully
recovered and has acted pretty respectable ever
since. It does any stream good to dam it now and
then when it refuses to perform its function.

Elmira barbers of that period were naturally English sym-
pathizers and they made no bones of displaying their ill-
feeling for the Yank, for the manner in which they went at
him with dull razors betokened as much. It was easily discernable that the Yankee patrons received less and much
inferior attention than the swaggering Englishman, but the
time arrived when these men of tonsorial art were glad to
become turncoats lest their business should suffer.

So when the gong proclaimed the dawn of Independence
and the Flag of Liberty floated over the conquered forts and
City Hall and Court House, an order was served on every
blooming British barber shop of the city to "get busy" under
penalty of confiscation and that very day marked the advent
of the barber pole.

Historians disagree as to the date of this important epoch,
so I can only add that it happened in Sullivan's time. The
shop figuring in this scene was later remodelled and is now
in the custody of Jones, Suter and Kahler, opposite Klapproth's Cafe, and Friend Metzger & Co's. market.

Chemung County is very much unlike any other county of the state. You will recognize it the moment you cross its border.

The engineer manages to break the good news to his sleeping passengers by hitting (about every 3 miles of the final run) one of those lovely birds of paradise commonly known as a "skunk" which never fails to bring the sleeper to his senses and warns him of his approaching destination.

Noticeable Symptoms of Temporary Insanity.

When one insists on telling a funny story while the host says grace.
When one eats soup with his fork.
And sponge cake with his spoon.
Picks his teeth with his index finger.
Blows his nose on his napkin.
Wipes his mouth on the table cloth.
And laps up the lemonade in the fingerbowl.

Linen collars should not be turned more than twice a week and cuffs reversed but once before consigning to the laundry.

E' PLEURISY   ONIONS

General Sullivan was a stern soldier with a gentle heart
as is shown in the following story told us by one who accompanied him on his campaign.

On one occasion, after a day of tedious battle and his
troops returned to camp tired and worn, he ordered a boun-
tiful supper prepared and bade them retire early that they
might avail themselves of all rest and recuperation possible,
then turning to his chambermaids he cautioned that part of
his household to go about the following morning's chamber
work with unusual care and quiet as he wished his men to
remain undisturbed till the toll of the last school bell. He also advised his trumpeter to "cut out" the reveille at break
of day and sent an orderly to the Bridge works to suggest
that its siren be silenced, for it robbed his sentinels and out-
posts of much needed sleep. All this Sullivan did and more,
too, that is why his men loved him and speak so well of
him now.

During the weary winter evenings after a hard day's battle,
the general would sit for hours beside his little oil stove
listening to that ever popular air, "Forty-Five Minutes from
Broadway," and dream of the lobsters a-la-Newburg, and
now and then would he feed those pleasant recollections with
a chunk of hard tack and jerked venison. At the same time
keeping his weather eye on the Indian situation and his frost
bitten ear in touch with his long distance telephone.

Never swear before a lady, unless of course, she is a notary
—even then, it would be advisable to refrain from uttering
the naked truth.

One dull and sluggish afternoon Sullivan (being somewhat worn by constant rest and repose) donned his accoutrements and allowed he (with a few warm personal friends) would call on the big red chief to invite his exeellency to participate in an impromptu athletic tournament. He found the great chief as host of a four o'clock tea in honor of a young buck who was just about to break into society. The chief, not expecting so vast a number of white guests, nor in fact did he expect any at all at that particular moment, was surprised to say the least and nonplussed to be sure, for he was prepared to feast and refresh only those of red skins, formally invited. So after an exchange of courtesies there began one of the bloodiest battles of the neighborhood, the chief's residence being on the very spot where now stands Frank A. Berner's delicatessen store. When the store was built it was necessary to remove the spot, though the very stones were used in the foundation of the present structure and much of the earth made into mortar. Thus endeth another chapter.

AUTHOR'S POSTSCRIPT.

It is not generally known that in the year 1877, the author had the pleasure of occupying (while in the employ of Brassington, the sign painter) a portion of three rooms over this very spot. Though the matter has been secretly guarded and kept from the public to save the structure from the ravages of relic hunters.—Hence his acute historical knowledge.

Philanthropy is a charming trait, but don't practice it on a weekly salary lest ye may soon need it practiced upon yourself.

ROSEWELL R. MOSS

Whose unbiased decisions in rendering judgment in daffydil cases have given this able jurist a world-wide reputation.

Police Justice's Special Notice.

We quote here a table of cut rates for the benefit of those who have transgressed and who for personal reasons have no desire to patronize their home justice of the peace:

First offense, to strangers $5.00
Second offense, six months with board and lodging

P. S.—Guests must come well recommended.

An attractive retreat is the State Reformatory —Exclusively for men. Guests from all parts of the State are accommodated at this hostelry. They arrive usually in personally conducted parties of twenty or thirty, accompanied by able and armed guides. As the road is narrow and the ascension up the hill difficult, a chain is attached to the ankle of each member to prevent mishaps. Many come and (owing to the comforts to be obtained therein) remain for years. The **suites** are rather cramped, though ample for light housekeeping for families of not more than two. Upon registering at the clerk's desk, guests are invited to deposit their valuables and partake of a sumptuous bath, a shave and a hair cut, and to facilitate matters in respect to introduction of one guest to another at their social functions, a number is given each of them in substitution of their proper names.

While sojourning at this resort one's habits become much changed, as it is compulsory to observe certain healthful rules, viz, early to bed and early to rise. Guests are cordially invited to participate in the various lines of manual training and to join the band or military organization of this exclusive place. The hotel can furnish accommodations to upwards of 1,300 guests and is usually filled to its capacity. If you contemplate an extended visit it would be well to wire for apartments in advance.

MASKOT OF THE ONCE CELEBRATED OVEN CLUB.

An old time structure down the river road known as Gerber's Brewery was burned some years ago and practically wound up the celebrated "Oven Club" whose annuals were pulled off in the adjoining woodland. Why this select body of business and professional men chose the environments of a brewery for their revelries is beyond my understanding. As a member of that respectable gathering I shall attempt to offer as an excuse the fact, that several of its oldest members were of German persuasion and slightly addicted to the beer habit. The rest of the club drank it purely out of sympathy for the brewer who was also a much beloved and addicted member of this society.

On these annual occasions a great feast was spread of pork and beans and other viands and onions in every conceivable style. In fact all the luxuries of the four seasons were embodied in the "menu" or "bill of fare." After the repast an innocent Sunday school game called "table stakes" was introduced by a few "well up" in the manipulation of the "deck," thus the balance of the day (and part of the night) was consumed.

Many of its one time members have crossed the border; some from over eating, others irretrievable bilious wrecks. The club is now but a pleasant memory. The brewery was razed by fire and the woodsman with his axe added the finishing touches.

As a harvesting center, Elmira stands among
the headliners. Much of the agricultural work is
performed by a society of that name, at its month-
ly meetings. It is the aim of this society to facilitate farming by handing out advice and figuring out future yields under certain soil and
weather conditions, and it frequently happens that
two crops of ice are harvested in one season without re-seeding. Farming has become so great a
science that it is no longer necessary to grip the
plow handles or swing the scythe. A knowledge
of arithmetic, a pad, a pencil and a lot of imagination is all that is needed to produce wonderful
crops.

Some men assume quite an independent swagger on a pal-
try fortune of fifty thousand. Bless their hearts! If all men
swaggered according to their wealth, this old globe would
rock so we should all be sea-sick.

Our newspapers are grand institutions. With out them we should not be reading daily weather quotations and planning (on the strength of their reliable forecasts) for a fishing trip on the promised calm and pleasant morrow, and finding two feet of snow and the juice in our thermometer frozen stiff instead. We should not be able to get our election returns before the vote is fairly cast, we should not have the pleasure of witnessing fresh, scalloped edge papers on our cupboard shelves every Monday or new dust lining beneath our parlor carpet every spring, were it not for that greatest of all institutions, the newspaper, They fill many voids besides those in the skull, even if one does not read. The bulk of paper in a Sunday issue is well worth the price of admission and he who kicks and finds fault in spite of the hundreds of benefits and comforts which are embodied in a Sunday edition should be classed among his ilk of the long ears.

It is every man's duty to believe in his home newspaper, just as devoutly as one believes in his religion, even if he doesn't actually believe in what he is believing. Newspapers don't die; when they make a statement it is absolutely so. If the weather is not as predicted, it is no fault of the papers but the fault of the weather for not adjusting itself to an honest prediction.

No siree! Without a newspaper, a brass band and a baseball nine you're simply "not in it."

Do you realize also that Elmira is the "Saratoga" of Chemung county? We have "Billy's" celebrated Breesport water which plays such an important part in the delightful summer game of High-Ball that its fame has spread far beyond the limits of its birthplace. If you are not already aware of this fact, it's high time you roll on over.

For lack of space we find it impossible for us to acquaint you with all its facts, particulars and

virtues. Permit us to introduce to you its present father and oxegenator, Wm. J. Lormore, who will tell you all about it.

Mrs. Mooney— and phwat do yez want wid the looking glass, Moike Mooney?

Mooney—Oi, want to foind out if its meslf oi brought home, or me frind Clancy.

Actress—(Tragically)—Leave the house sir!"

Burglar—(Politely)—Oh, certainly, I'll leave the house, all I want is just plain money and jewels.

It has been stated by some base person that Elmira is a suburb of Horseheads, but that is not so. The author having investigated the report thoroughly finds the statement closely approaching a bare-faced lie. Elmira is a city by itself and will allow none of equal size to knock the chip off her shoulder with impunity.

Many years ago there stood upon a spacious plot of ground surrounded by semi-tropical foliage such as greensward, dandelion and burdock, an ordinary looking edifice enclosed by an equally ordinary picket fence, an educational institution known as the Elmira Free Academy. A school of the highest order. A sort of finishing school where youths were prepared for a better and easier life. Many of Elmira's foremost business and professional men received their final touches at this institution and are now touching others, along life's rugged highway. It was deemed necessary in those days to encase every schoolhouse in some sort of a fence to prevent students from leaking out during recess, so the E. F. A. was no exception to the rule.

As we grow older we become more dignified of course. The school house that made great men of our fathers and grandfathers is no longer good enough for us. Time has changed our appetites for education and we must have all the unnecessary trimmings along with it. For this reason perhaps, the old red brick structure was wiped off the map and one more spacious and beautiful erected, yet the spelling books and arithmetics remained the same.

This beautiful and far superior structure was recently declared defective and unsafe, thus as this book is making its initial bow to the world, a third "Elmira Free Academy" is under way. "For the love of thy neighbor" who has eaten brick dust and ancient plaster with every meal since the first corner stone was laid, we implore thee to desist and let this last effort be permanent.

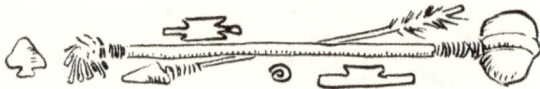

Elmira is the recognized home of fire engines. There is hardly a city in the United States that has not in its department one or more of the justly celebrated LaFrance machines. Next thing to a good reliable fire engine is an intelligent and well disciplined fire department. All of these things Elmira has, and a plenty. Only on rare occasions has it been necessary to call into action its auxiliary force which consists of the entire Horseheads department, its wives and children, aunts, uncles and cousins. Several times within the past generation when Elmira was threatened by a conflagration of unusual proportions and which required able council, the word was passed over the wire to wake up the wise and experienced heads of the village fire brigade and fetch them to the city, thus making Horseheads look more like a southward stampede than an ''Old Home Week'' celebration, for everything responded to Elmira's beck and call except household goods and first mortgages.

It is not my intention to point out the superior fire fighting qualities of a village department over that of a large city, but truly if you appreciate spectacular and heroic effects and wish the fire district to look as if a fire were really in progress, just turn the Horseheads auxiliary loose on it.

This is the recommend that Tony Romer gives the book: "By golly I don't belief von dam vord of it. Because Zim vas in Alsace ven der indians got shooted oud of Elmira, und besides he vasn't born already."

And the emphasis added to these remarks with his fist almost jarred the glasses off the table.

Hens should be compelled, by law, to lay one egg per day (barring Sundays, of course) so that a standard market price might be established upon her yearly output. Why should the hen be exempt from her rightful share of this world's burdens any more than the faithful mooly cow (who never skips a milking?)

We are already bedridden by fluctuations in our market quotations, and the sooner we rid ourselves of this abominable nuisance the better.

———— :-: ————

"Oh," exclaimed the new cider as it entered the bung hole of the old vinegar barrel, "I'm glad to see you, mother!"

Now Mr. Baseball Player. You did so well last season that
I have decided to reserve this space, in which to record your
conduct of 1912. If you make good your name shall go down
in posterity Do otherwise and your name is mud.

```
┌─────────────────────────────────┐
│        THIS SPACE               │
│     RESERVED FOR THE            │
│        PENNANT                  │
└─────────────────────────────────┘
```

TO THE E. W., L. & R. R. CO.

Many thanks for the oft repeated breakdowns
in your lighting system while our seven p. m. din-
ner (in its death chill) awaited us at the festive
board, for in leaving us in utter darkness on these
many occasions you have carried our thoughts
back to our dear grandmother, her sticky tallow
dips and smoky, odoriferous kerosene lamps.
Again, accept our unbounded gratitude.

Mamma, do kindly tell me what makes papa so glum.
'Tis but the lack of glimmer child, that makes your parent
glum.

REGARDING SWISS CHEESE

For the benefit of those of my readers who dote on Swiss Cheese, and know not why and whence come the holes therein, nor why Swiss Cheese bears such a striking resemblance to nothing else on earth, I, as a native of the Swiss Cheese belt, will endeavor to enlighten you, so far as my research, up to date, on that topic will permit me upon my honor to do.

Swiss Cheese is a bunch of holes made into the shape of an ordinary grindstone. Before pressing the cheese, a tasteless substance, made of goat's milk, is wrapped around each of the numberless holes, after which the holes are assembled and pressed into disc shape for consumption. The holes are raised only in Switzerland, a secret, jealously guarded by the Swiss government.

American cheese manufacturers have tried in vain to purchase holes of that Government, but alas, to allow the Yank into the secret of raising holes would mean ruin to the Swiss Nation, as the cultivation of holes for Swiss Cheese is its principal industry.

To back up my statements I can produce in evidence, my certificate of birth and the solemn word of honor of three Swiss warblers of my acquaintance.

ENFORCING THE LAW ON CODFISH BALLS.

THE BROOK TROUT VS. SALT COD.

Shall we discriminate between the brook trout and the noble Cod.

While every effort is put forward for the protection, preservation and propagation of the former, the docile Cod is allowed to lie dormant in some obscure corner grocery, unrecognized, unloved and uncovered.

The Salt Cod is not a game fish although his fragrance might suggest as much, "Be that as it may," we should try to better his condition. We should lessen our neglect of his royal Codship and see that laws are made for the protection of his descendant, "the succulent cod fish ball," which is so ruthlessly thrust upon the lunch counter. We should enforce said laws and run down the dastardly consumer, the free lunch fiend, whose gluttonous appetite leads him to conseal an extra supply of fish balls in his coat sleeve. Two fish balls of lawful size should constitute an allowance with one portion of beverage, and we should punish all violators brought within said law's jurisdiction regardless of sex, age, creed or color.

AN OLDTIME FRONTIER REMEDY.

Four yards of coiled hemp, one end carefully looped about the neck, and suspended from the lower limb of a nearby tree, so that the toes will clear the earth, will cure the most aggravated case of horse-stealing.

In some cases it is necessary to inject a dozen or more leaden pellets to make the cure speedy and effectual.

According to the prevalence of rats in women's hair there is much need of a "Pied Piper."

It is a great mistake to look upon life as a perfect hell. Hell is what we make it. We can make existence heavenly if we exercise sufficient determination. Now, for instance, nature endowed most of us with a pair of legs. They were intended as means of locomotion. If we use them properly and not excessively we add to our health, we sleep well, we eat well. Our arms were made to swing accordingly. To be able to use and appreciate these faculties is Heavenly.

But, suppose you have mortgaged your birthright to own a motor car, and you sit in it all day long, your feet on the lever and your mind on the wheel. Absorbed in grease and gasoline you see nothing but a whir of space, have no time to commune with nature or listen to the song of the heifer and the bellowing of the birds. And just as you think you are having the time of your life your tire flunks. That is "Hell!"

—————— :-: ——————

"FIRST AID" ADVICE.

One C. T. with a cherry stuck on the end of a sliver before breakfast, will sharpen the appetite of those who sat up all night with a sick friend.

"Ma," said the idol of the family, "what is a beautiful spectacle?"

"A circus parade, my darling, would be called a beautiful spectacle."

"Then I 'spose two circus parades would be a beautiful pair of spectacles."

MEMBERS OF THE GROTTO,

Please Take Notice!

That the foregoing High Sign recently adopted by the Horseheads "Blue" Lodge, is now a part of our work, and that it shall be the duty of every member of the Grotto to see that no violations (by the use of same) is permitted between the members of the "Eastern Star."

———:-:———

DRY READING

At best, history of any sort (dealing in cold facts as this does) becomes dry reading. To ease the sufferings of our readers we have allowed several local and some neighboring breweries to slip into our advertising pages. We should not be censured for this, however, as our columns are open to all who can produce the coin, whether it be kissed by saints or tainted by trusts, we can work it off on our grocer and butcher—have no fear.

———

Every man has his enemies. They are as essential to life as salt is to a hard boiled egg.

The man who tries to please everybody is a chump, for in pleasing everybody he really pleases nobody.

"Philo's Chicken College," a large and still growing institution, is one to which every Elmiran points with pride. It is a sort of breeding and training school for pullets and youthful roosters, where they are taught how to rear large families and to meet the responsibilities of life in general. No hen graduate from this institution has ever failed to find ready employment among the best families nor has ever a rooster bearing the "Philo Diploma of Good Breeding" gone forth into the world without meeting suitable and worthy helpmates. The college is on the Watkins car line in the outskirts of Elmira. Conductors will answer all questions bearing on this subject while passing that point.

An ex-drug clerk having accepted a position in a fish market and about to wait upon a lady customer—"Have you any 'Smelts?'" queried the customer. "Yes'm answered the ex-drug clerk, "which do you prefer, Jockey club, Heliotrope or musk?"— No bricks, please.

Mr. Roamabout—Good morning; is Mrs. Homebody in?
Green Servant—Yes sur, and no sur. She's in but she's out —I mane she's out of her clothes and in the bath tub—would you like to see her, sur?

As a comparison we show here an old mongrel bred who neglected to avail herself of the advantages of the Philo System—who selected her own (likewise mongrel) helpmate and did just as her will and fancy dictated. Observe the dif ference in the general aspect of both classes. The aristocrat- ic bearing of the Philo "Grads" and the abject poverty and inferiority of the other.

This old hen bore a family of ten—six of whom were bad eggs, monstrosities and idiots—and four died during the exciting period of childbirth.

"HELLO BILL!"

Assistant Chief Ellett handing out valuable information for the benefit of Foolish History.

For Sale on Easy Terms.

A wooden leg seven years of age, sound except one knot-hole 1-2 inch in diameter nearly healed up with putty. Its owner wishing to give up a lucrative business to invest capital in real estate. Also a pair of green goggles and a sign to match with the words "Please Help the Blind."

Yep! Pa went to Noo York to look over some fancy stock. He writ ma that he kum acrost a fine pair of pulletts on Broadway but the price was so steep he couldn't afford to buy'm. He's goin' to stay over another nite and perhaps he kin land 'em.

He says he's glad ma didn't kum with him 'cause Noo York is such a fast and wicked place he'd much rather be at prayer-meeting. I hope he buys the pulletts, I'd take one off'n his hands.

These is pa's pullets.

The inconsistency of man's ways applies to the husband who has just been out with the boys and spent 75 cents per round for the drinks, then complains because his wife has invested in two dozen fresh eggs when the price is 5 cents a dozen higher than usual.

Grasshopper Hill earned its proud title about A. D., 1860 after a prolonged siege by the peaceable farmers of the western uplands of Horseheads, against the six legged pest. The battle (in every particular) resembled that of historic "Waterloo," and as the grasshopper (like the noble Duke of Wellington) held his grass to the last hopper. It was only natural that his descendants should build a monument, such as England erected to her beloved fighting duke.

This monument is easily discernable by means of the naked eye, during the months of July and December and may be seen from trains passing through the locality. Don't miss seeing this famed attraction.

MIKEOVITCH O'HOOLIGANSKI.

A Russian nobleman, who single-handed with his trusty pick, hacked one thousand brawny redskins to bits, then proclaimed himself the first mayor of Grasshopper Hill.

My Gracious!
Thats a "Bumm"
weed, Quoth the General
• As he Tackled a wad of
Big-Flats Tobacco.

Experience and close observation convince us
that tobacco is rather an uncertain and unsafe
crop to meddle with. Especially so was that of
the season of 1911, when early frost overtook
much of the weed ere it could don its winter "Havana Wrapper" or crawl into the hot licorice vat.
Little thought do we give (as we gnaw at that un-
couth slab of pressed foliage with the fancy
name) to the nights of anguish endured by the
grower of said leaf while rearing that delicate article. Did we but understand the dangers and
hardships from the elements the plant itself en-
counters as it slowly and tediously approaches
the age of cigarhood we would, no doubt, treat it
with greater reverence than is now the case. We
would perhaps remove it from our lowly and vul-
gar hip pocket and assign it a place of honor
above our heart, beside (its brother) the pipe and
our spectacle case, nor would we allow it to pass
into the hands of Tom, Dick and Harry, at the
mere request for "a chaw of yer sole leather."
We would remind our cronies that even plug tobacco when duly christened is entitled to respect.

Though the country was new and grubbing was
hard at the close of the revolution, many soldiers
preferred to tender their resignations by mail
rather than face honorable discharge, and immediately took to the woods, where tracts were
cleared and settlements started—"Latta Brook",
"Holderman's Holler" and Tompkins' Corners—
being three of the many localities where the
thrift of civilization faces one from every point
of the compass. If you have an auto, or can borrow your neighbor's, it would pay you to make a
trip over the spots mentioned, to see for yourself
what the war of the revolution has done for history.

ELDRIDGE PARK.

A charming spot of which Elmira should feel proud. Folks from afar go there for rest and recreation and return home tired and weary. The park is at the disposal of all who can reasonably behave themselves. It was laid out many years ago by an enterprising citizen—Dr. Eldridge by name—whose sole ambition it was to give others enjoyment at his personal expense.

It nestles comfortably between two trunk line railroads over whose tracks more than four million trains pass per day. It contains a lake of some dimensions, with a broad and beautiful drive bordering its entire circumference, where, if in the mood, one may leisurely drive, walk or scamper, and listen to bands, engine bells and shrill whistles, all of which lend a sort of mellowness to the summer atmosphere. In another portion of the park may be seen an enclosure in which venison is nursed until it reaches the age of self-support. It is then allowed to seek the freedom of the forest and shift for itself.

A Cannibal King after looking into our laws and habits reckoned that civilization was all right, (when stewed down in a kettle and well seasoned).

Smoke the "ZIM" Cigar. A hero medal presented with every box. They are made by a big gun by the name of Cannon. He assumes all risks so I feel safe in recommending them to my friends.

The Zim Cigar contains no leather shavings, no chewing gum wads, no curled hair, nor other odorous matter. Only tobacco of the highest grade, carefully selected and rolled into form by lily white hands, each and every coil having been thoroughly scrutinized and subjected to acid tests by an efficient officer of the Board of Health.

LEWIS E. MOSHER

Attorney—Orator

Statue of "Hank" Clay, advising him to seek an honest vocation and avoid the pedestal of fame.

Although Mr. Mosher's fame has not yet reached the point where his name would be of commercial value to the cigar trade (as in the case of the lamented Henry Clay) such a fate is but a question of time.

In producing a work of this sort which deals with individuals in the light of ridicule, there is often danger that some of the victims may perish while the work is in progress and too far advanced to admit of any changes being made. It behooves a caricaturist, therefore, to select only men of rugged constitutions, as the shock may prove too severe and terminate fatally.

As a safeguard against possible calamity, we have retained a corps of physicians to ascertain the exact degree of endurance of our intended victims before the artist begins his deadly work.

Battles are oft times lost through lack of rigid discipline.
This fact General Sullivan impressed very forcibly upon the
minds of his fellow officers, who likewise proceeded to im-
press it upon the minds of their subordinates and therein
lies the whole secret of his success. This picture by the way,
was made from a war correspondent's description.

At the close of hostilities, when the thirteen Stars and as
many Stripes were substantially spiked to the Liberty Pole,
Washington wired Sullivan for information regarding the
changes desired in our public affairs. "Give us a Rural Free
Delivery," replied Sully, for then the lazy lubbers who till
(or don't till) the soil may be spared the trouble of coming to town for the family mail and bringing home to their
beloved wives a "souse" instead. Immediate steps were
taken to establish an R. F. D. and a century and a quarter
later finds us enjoying this luxury. Thanks to those two
great minds, Washington and Sullivan.

WANTED—A young man to act as distributor of daily output of counterfeiting plant; must be silent, conservative, energetic and daring. One of experience as a clever crook preferred. Salary $500.00 per month.

Father—Tommy, why don't you mind your mother?

Tommy—Cos I want to let her see there's one male in the house who has a mind of his own.

The ingenuity displayed by some men to beat the bartender out of a drink is wonderful. Here is an instance which comes within the realm of truth, as it occurred in Horseheads (where never a lie was uttered:)

Kelly—"How mooch do oi owe yez Jerome?"

Jerome—"Forty cents Mr. Kelly."

Kelly—Agitating a bunch of keys in his pocket—"Thot's correct Jerome—forty cints it iz? Well give me a drink of the bist whishkey in the house," (still jingling his keys, which sounded to the bartender like ready money)

Kelly—After gulping down four fingers and setting the empty glass on the bar remarks with emphasis "NOW! Remember! Ut's fifty cints I owe yez."

LOWMANVILLE.

Another station once in the bloody realm and infested by savages is now a peaceable settlement. And where once stood the wigwams of hostiles, there now exist two important elements of milk punch. A dairy and a still, which stand within easy access of each other, are among its principle industries. Had the Indian foreseen the future of the place, he might have been induced to settle down to private life and share with us the fruits of civilization.

FRANK ARMITAGE
The "Great Westerner."

Who declares that, to be healthy all the time, one should drink "Great Western" and no other. Splendid advice. We shall leave our cellar door ajar, perhaps a case of the favorite prescription may walk in without knocking.

Like all good and well bred cities, Elmira has several fine banks. They are handy institutions, where a man's word of honor (penned above his signature and endorsed by a friend of means) is readily accepted on loans, not exceeding the capital stock of said banks and six per cent legal interest deducted in advance for accommodations. It is policy to "stand in" with the officers of these institutions, for in such case the transaction can be "pulled off" with greater ease.

If you have been indiscreet in your expenditures or living beyond your salary and your creditors are pushing you, take your hard luck story to the kind hearted president of one of these charitable institutions. He will do the rest.

"Oh madam," remarked a half-frozen tramp to an old maid, "Have you any old clothes that you could spare me?"

"Well, I fear sir, mine wouldn't fit you," said the old maid, blushingly, "But here are a pair of suspenders my brother cast aside this morning."

A NEW COUNTERSIGN FOR THE ODD FELLOWS.
(Patent Under Consideration).

By this method, without the usual grips or password one may determine whether he is in the company of fellow craftsmen. A simple movement of the legs, which means, "Are youse Odd Fellows?" and the linking of the legs of your new acquaintances means "We is!" after which all are at liberty to dwell freely on lodge matters.

"Corporal!" commanded the General, "take a detachment of picked men, two in number, (including yourself) and proceed by way of trolley westward to Water and Lake streets, thence dispatch one of said number northward as far as 'Falseys Bar.' Let him hold that position until approached by a native wearing a friendly face and white apron and to him deliver that bucket with this countersign, viz: 'One pint and charge it.' Then let him report to me at once for I am as dry as a herring."

"I command you also, Corporal, to bear to me in person the chosen date for the next 'Hassenpfeffer' blowout at Billy Maurer's, for I wish to concentrate my forces in that vicinity, as a safeguard against hostile interference during the contemplated feast. I trust you see the point, Corporal, now off with your command and see that my orders are executed with despatch.

The close of the Revolution threw many an able bodied red man upon his own limited resources. To eke out a livelihood in white man fashion (until death by natural causes should overtake them) was indeed degrading and humiliating to these-one-time nobles, and many were the grumblings of discontent for the shabby treatment accorded them by the British government. Being now without home, food or funds, they reluctantly assumed the white man's burden while the sheriff seized their real estate and the instalment man their paintings, carpets and furniture.

AN INFALLIBLE RECEIPT

For those who wish to prolong life 1,000 years.

NEVER worry about your miserable self.

NEVER worry about the misery of others.

NEVER worry about your debts, let your administrators do it.

NEVER worry about the comments and criticisms of your neighbors.

NEVER put yourself to any inconvenience to accomodate others.

NEVER subscribe to any local or other charities.

NEVER drink at your own expense.

NEVER give up your seat to women in a street car.

SPONGE all your reading.

BORROW all you can; lend nothing.

TAKE the biggest half of everything and the best seat in the house.

KICK on everything that is done for your comfort and make others as miserable as possible.

KNOCK everybody and point to yourself as the real "IT" and long life will be yours.

Types of the latter day Indians.

ARTHUR T. LOSIE
The Biggest Buck at the Elk Ranch.

Boys enlisting in the Army should enlist as officers at the outset, as it has been shown that Epaulettes are a great protection against rheumatism which is so prevalent in the ranks, owing to exposed shoulders which are at the mercy of the chilly rains. The brass, or gold plated Epaulettes offer a sort of shelter and eve trough.

'OH! LISTEN TO THE BAND.'

Elmira is a musical centre. It can boast of more brass bands to the square inch than any city of its size in or out of the state. After the Civil war, Asa La France started the ball rolling which finally suffered a slump until the latter end of the Seventies, then the reorganization of the La France band took place, with Joe Benjamin as its gorgeous drum-major. This band was called the Golden Slipper band in honor of its first effort: "Oh, dem golden slippahs." Today we have brass bands galore. There are men among us who make the organizing of bands a steady business and as soon as the recruits are able to push wind into their horns, these promoters leave us to suffer alone. It should be embodied in the contract that said person remain on the job and be compelled to listen, night after night, to his dastardly work, until the "wind jammers" reached a reasonable state of perfection. The worn-out Phonograph record is bad enough, but the promiscuous organizing of brass bands in civilized communities is the limit. "Gentlemen, be merciful!"

E.M.BIEN, PRES.   J.P.KOPF, TREAS   S.B.KISTLER, SEC'Y.

EXECUTIVE OFFICERS OF FAMOUS GROTTO BAND

These gentlemen have a remarkable ear for music and are the principle cause of all the noise.

"YOU DON'T SAY SO!"

"SAY PA! I WANT TO FIGHT THE BRITISH AND THE INDIANS WHEN I GET BIG!"

WASHINGTON'S EARLY PREDICTIONS.

The Youthful George Washington, after telling the truth about the cherry tree, warned his venerable pa, to be prepared for the worst, as he anticipated serious trouble with the Tories and Indians up in the Chemung Valley and that Skinny Sullivan, a neighbor's kid, had promised that he, before many changes of the moon, would go out there and clean house for them. His father was amazed, for, knowing Georgie's veracity to be beyond questioning he doubted him not. And it is a remarkable fact that everything passed off just as he predicted.

On a certain A. M., (the date of which for professional reasons we withhold) and just as the Yankees' breakfast bell was about to announce the morning meal, the British, scantily clothed in a dense fog, were observed evacuating towards the Erie R. R. station. Sullivan, though still itching for another kick into the bosom of King George's Knickerbockers, decided to curb his ire and otherwise control his feelings lest they miss their train, likewise their ship that was to convey them back to the land of their birth.

Gen. Sullivan's division was ushered into battle by the famous "Palmer's Continental Drum Corps," which sent the spirit of Seventy-Six coursing through the arteries of rank and file, and goaded them on to ultimate victory. To this celebrated body of musicians is due much of the glory of the conquest of the Chemung Valley.

The unveiling of the first Indian statue should not be allowed to go unmentioned, as it cut quite a gash in the Sullivan period and marked an epoch which might well be termed the Wooden Indian Era.

Extract from oration delivered at the unveiling by one of Elmira's foremost Sons of Oratory:

We are gathered here, my friends, (and others) to unveil and do honor to this beautiful chunk of hemlock timber and to welcome the coming of the 5c perfecto. It is said that the only good Indian is the dead Indian. That, my friends, is hardly so, as we all must agree that the best Indian is our friend here, the wooden Indian, for in him we have absolutely nought to fear and in this state he is far more welcome in our community than either the live or dead one. Let us hope that all future Indians shall be borne to us by slow freight and made of similar material as our friend on this pedestal, and if killing must be done, let us trust to the virtues of the cheap cigar to fulfill the mission of the tomahawk.

The "Kings Own" of Canada, a regiment of kilties which was uncermoniously banished from Chemung county for violations of social etiquette, inasmuch as they persisted (contrary to the city ordinance) in fighting in their "bear skins.". This picture shows a section of same, passing a given point in disrupted order and in much haste.

It was largely through the efforts of the Barbers' & Hair Cutters' Union that Washington sent Sullivan on his mission of mercy. The fact is, the Indians were doing much pernicious scalping in and about Elmira which threatened demoralization to the hair cutting trade, and it was only to avoid utter ruin that the movement against the Indians was planned and executed.

If Washington was the original inventor of Washington pie then he is alone to blame for the dark and gloomy blot cast upon his good name, but if he did not invent it then he who was guilty of building so vile a monument to the memory of so great a man should dwell in perdition. Washington pie is a mass of the stale stuff of the bakery, made into pulp and were if not for the hand full of currants and raisins and cheap brown sugar or molasses added it would taste less palatable than common bar soap. Can you, then imagine anything more unfit to bear the noble name of Washington than this alleged pie. I once made Washington pie for three years, according to the accepted formula and I have seen much of it devoured, but in all my experience, the only person I ever met who could digest the aforesaid with any degree if ease and comfort and without the use of explosives, was a certain night watchman, and he said he ate it to give him courage, for after tackling the pie he was ready for any emergency. Poor fellow is now where all pie eaters go and may his soul rest in peace, for I know his finish must have been sad and terrible.

An old proverb says that "The world owes every man a living." That may be true, but many have gone to jail in trying to collect the debt.

Obscure words or phrases used by the author are defined in this column, viz:

SOUSE—Meaning a load of Peaches, borne within the body and sometimes causing blind staggers.

A LOAD OF PEACHES—A term used to express the condition of one wearing a "Jag."

JAG is also expressed by the word "Bunn," according to the best authority.

JOHNNY FRIEND

Dwelling Upon the Indian Situation.

HON. DR. R. P. BUSH (Assemblyman) CHAMPIONING THE
CAUSE OF THE CODFISH BALL.

It is a well known fact that Sullivan became very tired of
the monotony of settling disputes with arms and sent one
of his trustiest officers under a flag of truce, to confer with
the Indian chief on the advisability of "pulling off" one of
their scraps on the gridiron. The Red warrior readily accepted Sullivan's challenge and both sides proceeded to select their toughest football timber, and secure the ball
grounds for that purpose. Sullivan realizing his weakness
owing to the lack of experienced rooters, and feeling the
absolute necessity of that indispensible element wired a special request to Cornell for the loan of one hundred of its
huskiest students for the occasion. The result you already
know and which is written in history as the Massacre of
Miller's Creek.

Bum Actor—Why, one time I was with Booth.
Theatrical Manager—You should be with him now.

Kind Lady—Is it not possible for you to leave liquor alone?
Tramp—No, madam! I have a weak heart and it requires liquor to sustain heart action.

Wiggins—Did that airship you invested in so heavily prove worthless?
Higgins—Oh, not entirely—It killed the inventor.

Friend—Have you got down to eating in a ten cent lunch room?
Poet—Got down to it? Why, great scott! I have been working months to get up to it.

DEWITT C. DECKER
Custodian of the Chemung River, in one of his mild but threatening attitudes of authority.

A BIT OF EVERYTHING

The wealth of the Rockerfellers or the Hair Tonics of the world would not grow a spear of hair on John D.'s bald head, yet he can, without the use of a single cent or a drop of tonic raise hair on the heads of his employees at a moment's notice.

Biggs—Why did your cashier leave you?
Banker—I must have been too heavy to carry off. The safe and myself is all he did leave, though.

Tom Kat—There Maria, I've followed your advice and got my nine lives insured in nine different companies.

Husband—That can't be her own hair Mrs. Frills is wearing
Wife—Well, it is, for I was with her when she bought it.

Mother—Euclid, do you love papa or mamma best?
Little Euclid—I shant tell 'till you gimme another piece of pie.
Mother—(Emphatically)—No sir! You can't have another piece of pie.
Euclid—(Pouting)—Well then, I love both of you, but I think papa is more generous and has the best disposition of the two.

Men may come and men may go, but the flying machine is here for keeps.

One very remarkable trait in General Sullivan, which is not usual in public men, he absolutely refused to be interviewed by newspaper reporters and declined to dwell either upon himself or his achievements.

"WHO SAID RATS?"

County Fairs are indispensable for they bring the farmer annually face to face with himself and give him an opportunity to cuss the laws of York state for abolishing the canteen from Fair grounds. But if he be observing, he may notice now and then a group of parched pilgrims in quest of the Guiding Star to lead them to the spot where, buried deep beneath the carpet of a horse's bed chamber, there reposes a quart of the forbidden juice and if he be a wise one he will follow that Guiding Star.

CHAS. SNYDER
Keeper of the Elk House.

R. T. LEWIS

Or the "Man-With-Big-Hat," as the Indians would call
him. Can build bridges, run a Sunday school or a prize fight.
In short, he is what we should call a versatile man and a
good mixer.

In the presence of corpslike silence, under cov-
er of a dense moonlight and escorted by continental troops, an equipage bearing the first consign-
ment of national currency entered the lower city
gates on its weary way to the "Chemung Canal
Bank" with which to redeem important paper
bearing General Sullivan's autograph.

One of the first moves in General Sullivan's advance was to inquire into the health of the hostile Indians, finding many suffering from sore throats, he at once arranged to cut off their supply of Joe Benjamin's Cough drops by sending his advance agent to buy up the entire stock of his six-by-nine factory. It might have been a strategic military move on the part of Sullivan, but it was the means of spreading the cough habit broad cast—that even to the present day we are compelled to cough up for everything to sustain life and to keep body and soul together.

RAY TOMPKINS

Shouldering the Worry and Cares of Life.

July and August are the months we have set aside for our annual torture (camp life.) Those are the months we proceed to expose our rich flesh and blood to the insect world and make martyrs of ourselves in general. Should our wives or hired girls dare offer us (at home) the food we eat and relish in camp, it would certainly mean their finish. Yet withal we imagine we are having a "Bully" time.

And then

While in the throes of camping bliss
We write such blooming rot as this:

MY OWN CHEMUNG

Especially Dedicated to the Locality of Big Flats, N. Y.

I love thy stream from shore to shore,
    Thy charms shall lure me evermore,
Thy bass who lie out in thy stretch
    I angle for but never catch,
I grope around for Mama's bread,
    But find some mice got there ahead,
Black ants in everything I eat
    And red ones too in all that's sweet.
Thy frogs that croak and groan all night,
    Raccoons that roam in thy soft twilight,
The music of thy rattlesnake
    Add much to keep my thoughts awake.
Thy pesky skeeters, just a few
    The odor of a Pole Cat too.
Ten days and nights of joyous cheer
    And rheumatiz the rest of the year,
For joyful misery, without a doubt
    There's NIX compares with camping out.

CAGEHILL SOCIETY PERSONALS

(By Charlie Pickerpocket)

Inmate No. 496½X—Entertained a few friends in solitary confinement at whist Saturday P. M., while the guards were off duty.

Inmate No. 64XP¼—Has left the Awkward Squad and will be seen hereafter among the ranks bearing a wooden gun.

Inmate No. 29GH63½—Is preparing to leave the locality "incognito". A file was presented to him on his last birthday by a small army of friends on the outside together with railroad maps, time tables and valuable advise for his future welfare.

Inmate No. 1½09G—The Hack Saw artist has done some wonderfully clever work with that instrument of late. He cut away three two-inch steel bars in a single night without detection. A feat never before equalled—he left no word nor address.

Inmate No. 3369A—Received honorable mention and recommended to a lower grade in recognition of his talent in quilt tying and wall scaling.

Inmate No. 567WX—Is trying out his runabout which he picked up in the city while on parole.

Inmate No. 1110PQ—Would like to correspond with someone well up in crooked work in the hope of forming a co-partnership to follow fairs and circuses.

Inmate No. 3X157—Has completed his contract and will give up his apartments on Tier Three and return to his former home in the South.

Dress parade and band concerts every afternoon in the plaza at 4:30. Curfew at nine sharp.

— ⊶✪⊷ —

"Doc, I wish you'd give me something to cure my cold."

"Have you taken anything at all for it?"

"Only a prescription that Widow Jones knew was good for it and some pills Bill Brown gave me what he was sure would fix me up and a dose of rhubard tea Mrs. Bixon made for me and a cough mixture invented by Davy Hiller and a mustard sweat and ginger poultice and——"

"Hold on! You don't want a doctor, its an undertaker you need—he's two blocks below."

The "Red Jacket Glee club" rehearsing a new "War Whoop" composed by that celebrated lyrist, Chas. X. O'Brien, which was later introduced at a surprise party to General Sullivan.

HOW TO MAKE GRANDMOTHER'S OLD FASHIONED PRUNE PIE

FIRST:—Set the kerosene oil can upon the kitchen table, then pit one-half pound of stewed prunes; fill the lamps, and put into the prunes one heaping handful of granulated sugar, and wipe the soot off the chimneys. Add the juice of two lemons, trim the wicks and roll out the crust quite thin —wipe the oil off the bottoms of lamps and crimp the edges of crust with thumb and first finger.

Judge—What was the charge the last time you were here?
Brannigan—Foive dollars, yer honor.

THE AUTHOR'S EVENING PRAYER.

Go forth little Book and perform thy glad mission
And bear me the fruit ($) that betters my condition.
AMEN!

The retail price of this work is 50c in American money,
2¼ francs in French money; 2¼ Mark in German money,
and a "Hell-of-a-dollar" in Jewroosalem mazooma.
Fresh butter and eggs taken in exchange.

I wish to state that the less you believe in this book and
the more you criticize and comment upon the statements
herein the better I shall like it, for in that event I am as-
sured of a large sale. There is nothing more successful than
an assertion which gives rise to doubt, and of these this book
contains many. I feel sure this work will never become a
part of our educational system so I have spared no pains in
bending the truth a bit in every instance.

We wish to extend our heartfelt thanks to the kindly disposed friends who so generously added to our sorrows and
sufferings, by their many foolish suggestions, during the sad
hours of publication. Also to our beloved neighbors who,
against many protestations, persisted in neglecting their
household duties to aid us in uniting these pages and covers, and to others who, by their deeds and acts, displayed
a personal interest in our business and private welfare. May
a kind providence guide them in overcoming their innocent faults, is the sincere hope of the
AUTHOR
PRINTER
and
BINDER.

ROY SMITH

The Maker of Big Cities

When Roy cuts loose he can make as much noise as a full brass band.

————:-:————

Do you recall the story of "Hank" Whitney (Eli Woodchuck) of more than a quarter of a century ago? How Eli sprang into fame in a single day while helping to move a stove down a flight of stairs and at the summons of the fire bell "Hank" dropped his burden (kabang!!) and fled where duty called him. From that moment Hank was a noted figure and enjoyed unusual privileges ever after. A similar incident occurred when Bill Ellet bounced out of a barber chair half shaven, with lather and towels streaming, to answer the call to fire duty. But Bill never got half the glory out of it that Hank did, because his was a paid job, and to the admirers of Eli, it appeared as if "Bill" were emulating the noble deeds of the lamented "Eli" to cop the laurels from the brow of Hank the late volunteer.

That was when Dan Richardson played with the Pickaways and Jessie Gibbons slammed the cymbals in the LaFrance band and many, quite many years before Elmira attained its Fifty Thousand population mark.

Speaking of the Cymbal blower of a band, I regard him as the greatest acquisition to such an organization. . He wields greater power even than the leader, insomuch as he covers up most of the frightful noises emanating from the horns, therefore when you listen to a band's discourses and the cymbals dominate, you may be sure that the music is "punk" and the cymbal slammer is trying to save the band from utter disgrace.

MALONEY & MARSHALL

The cars do move some when this bunch gets after them.

Inasmuch as it is the rule to offer premiums to
boom a new literary work we have arranged with
two reliable institutions and offer the following
premiums, viz:

To the first cash purchaser who dares to find
fault with his purchase, a bed in the Arnot Ogden
Hospital (gratis).

To the man or woman who spent their last shil-
ling for our benefit, a life membership in the
Breesport County house.

MANAGER NORTON

Of The Lyceum Theatre
Up to his old tricks of palming off box seats on
his friend, the author.

ON MARRIAGE.

Our present matrimonial system will never receive my sanction until some of its weak spots are repaired and amendments added that will fetch it beyond the limits of a bunco game.

When you enter into a horse deal you are usually made acquainted with the animal's unpleasant points, and you buy him with your eyes wide open to every blemish and fault in his beastly nature. But when a father hands you his only daughter at the altar, does he warn you of her cold feet and her unheavenly snore, and that she wears hip pads and false hair? No, he does not, because he's only too eager to shift her off his hands. Yet this deception is lawful and binding. Is it a wonder that bridegrooms look so sour at the end of their honeymoon, when they have finished their inventory of her and her acquisitions, and later ask for a decree for false representation?

All of this could be obviated by a few words added by the minister: "Do you take her as she stands, with all her false hair, hip pads, snores, cold feet, and other blemishes"? Then if you are chump enough to say "I do!", your punishment will be well merited.

MYRON T. BURNS

Better Known as Burns, the Squab Man.

FRANK TRIPP

**And the Humorous Pup that Growls Every Saturday
Afternoon.**

————: :————

    The story of a man who committed suicide and left a note asking the police authorities to please pardon him for using a gun without a license finds its parallel in a story of a farmer who hailed a passing funeral procession and requested permission to put a couple of cans of milk inside the hearse and wouldn't the undertaker be kind enough to stop on his way to the cemetery and leave them at the creamery and get a receipt for same, thus saving him an extra trip for which he'd be much obliged.

Very many years ago there lived in the City of Elmira a
man who could neither read nor write, yet he conducted a
grocery and general store and most of his customers were of
the "Please charge it" sort.   It was the habit of this particular grocer, when entering a sale upon his books to make a
crude drawing of the article sold on credit.   One day a patron dropped in to balance his account and was surprised to
find himself charged up with a cheese—indicated by a circle.
"Why," said the patron, "I never bought a whole cheese in
my life."   "Well, you certainly did," answered the grocer in
warm language, "for here is a circular mark on your page
which means a cheese."   "Are you sure it wasn't a grindstone"
ejaculated the patron.   "Oh by jove," said the grocer, "so it
was, but I forgot to put the hole in it."

Klapproth waiting for the mercury to reach the Atlantic
City point.   This picture was made in February, 1912, hence
the absence of the straw bonnet.

ATTENTION FIREMEN !

Don't forget that the annual parade of the Guinn Guinnip Fire department will be held late in the summer, at the rear of Ed. Warner's Grocery. Fire works in the evening—pipes and tobacco. Election of officers for the ensuing year. The Exempts will participate.

SWAT THE FLY AND SAVE THE CHILD.

The fly crusade will begin with the approach of warm weather. It is every mother's duty to protect the life and health of her infant, also the comfort of the bald headed end of the family. The cost of living is greatly increased by the pilferings of this annoying and dangerous pest, so get busy and practice the upper-cuts, body-blows, half-Nelsons and other scientific movements with the fly-swatter.

—————:-:—————

We need no calendar to warn us when summer is here, for that is the time when our dear wife unties a fresh box of "Tanglefoot" flypaper and begins to distribute its adhesive contents broadcast, from the kitchen table to the piano, and from the furnace room to the guest chamber.

Sticky fly-paper is an ornament to any household, I will admit, but it should be kept where the house cat can't roll itself up in it, or where the seat of (the household) government will not come in contact with same, for it is a beastly disease when once it gets a hold on you. We do not love the fly, that is sure, but we hesitate not in saying that we love sticky fly-paper much less.

——•▢•——

Trout fishing is one of the dominating spring sports of Chemung County. To experience the exhilarating effects in full measure one should select a stream running through pasture fields recently posted, containing an ugly bull and surrounded by a barbed wire fence.

ED CROWELL

When a mere boy he used to hold the skein of
yarn for his grandmother to wind into a ball, thus
Ed soon became an adept hand at knitting—in
fact he knits the kind that never wears out.

The Caricaturist never fears the
man he ridicules, but his wife is the
one who passes judgment which is
either the making or undoing of him.
I would ask the dear wives whose beloved husbands appear in this book,
to bear up and be as generous as becomes their loving nature.

Cravats slid around under the left ear, look very chic
and develish.

COLONEL SCOTT

Hello! The Kernel is in town again with his inseparable companion the big stick.

————————:-:————————

The human family is a generous race. It has formed societies for the equal distribution of sympathy, sometimes it is well bestowed and oftentimes not. But sympathy doesn't feed the hungry nor clothe the destitute. Take the case of Adam and Eve for instance, when the avenging angel drove them from their game and fruit preserve, into the cold macadamless highway, without a penny in their pockets nor even an extra fig leaf, that they might at least have a change of garment on wash day. Then was the time and opportunity for some charity or missionary society to perform good and noble work, but none came forward to relieve their distress. Adam, the poor fellow, was obliged to break ground anew, without credit or financial standing whatsoever; with naught but a shaggy growth of embryo whiskers to shield his shame from the public gaze. And poor Eve's Paris gown was anything but becoming to a decent lady. Sick over the recent loss of a shortrib and humiliated beyond expression, Adam's new domestic life was not very pleasant.

They were our nearest kin, yet when they needed succor we gave them a frigid "turn down". But such is the disposition of the human race. We are quite apt to shower empty sympathy upon the shivering and hungry family of our own neighborhood, and money and clothing upon the dark skin heathen in some tropical climate.

W. O. CREW
President of The Business Men's Association

The smile that made Elmira famous. Mr. Crew's smile is
the kind that never wears off. The sort that puzzles the most
expert gambler. It seems to say: "I've got five aces, what
have you got?"

Mothers, before mending the pants of their
youthful sons are quite apt to dump the pockets of
their contents and in many cases cast away the
rubbish which the boy has faithfully accumulated
between school hours. They forget that the rusty
nails, bits of cord, marbles, chalk, etc., are his sole
stock in trade—his total asset, as it were—each
having its intrinsic value in making swaps with
other boys. Encourage him in his enterprise and
you may develop in him a foremost junk dealer.
Discourage him and you may blight his business
instincts forever.

TRUE DEFINITIONS.

RAZOR—A sharp edged implement used for opening oysters and sardine boxes, and sometimes for cutting corns.

TOOTHBRUSH—A small ivory handled affair with pigs bristles growing out of one end, sometimes used for scrubbing celery and for cleaning teeth the rest of the time.

SHEARS—Two blades riveted together, used for cutting tin and wire nails; used also as tack puller and screw driver.

FORK—A thing with a handle on it and three sharp points used for picking the teeth at the table and for pulling corks out of catsup bottles.

CUSPIDORE—A handy vase-like jar made to stumble over in the dark.

TACK—A dainty article made to step on at night when the baby is teething.

OIL CAN—Sometimes used to hide molasses away from children.

Sufficient margin has been left around pages for the ac-commodation of notes, memorandas, and autographs. It would not be out of place to add cooking recipes, as every kitchen (without a doubt) will contain one of these books in course of time.

The price of this book is within the reach of the poorest nation on earth, so there is no excuse for excluding it from the National Libraries of the world.

ASTRONOMICAL OBSERVATIONS FOR 1913

If the moon is in its accustomed position at 9 p. m., Dec. 31st., it is an unfailing sign that Jan. 1st. will follow within three hours and one minute.

KEY TO TYPOGRAPHICAL ERRORS.

The word "die" on page 30, referring to our newspapers should read "lie.". We have adopted this simple method of after-explanation to do away with the task of proof-reading.

"UNCLE SAM" TABER

Once owner, proprietor, editor and pressman of the "Horse-heads Philosopher." When Sullivan had finished his work of perforating Indians, Sam was selected to print their of-ficial obituaries and in that capacity became quite noted.

Besides he had a knowledge of law which afforded him ad-mission to practice at every bar in Chemung and Schuyler counties.

JOHN M. CONNELLY
President, Chamber of Commerce
John has wielded the bung starter for seven
consecutive years and is good for seven more

————:•:————

ABOUT PHOTO AND CARICATURE

While groping about for a plausible excuse to
offer the readers for a number of unrecognizable
portraits in this book, I can think of no one more
deserving of the blame than the photographer.

It is the photographer's business to flatter his
subject, while the caricaturist reaches out in the
opposite direction. In plain words the photographer by retouching negatives eradicates the
lines and blemishes which are of great value to
the caricaturist, thus sacrificing truth for beauty,
to gratify one's vanity. The caricaturist sacrific-
es beauty for truth, and often gets cussed for his
pains.

As a rule man's horror for the photo gallery
equals that of the dentist's chair. The torture is

less painful, no doubt, but the effect upon the
nerves—"Dear-me-sus." For instance, the moment you enter a photo studio a certain chemical
odor permeates your system, a peculiar unexplain-
able feeling of fear assumes charge of you. You
sit down amid heart palpitation and failing breath
while the lens is being focused, then your head
is tenderly placed into a vise to retain its unnat-
ural posture and your eyes become fixed upon
some object until they are ready to burst from
their sockets. At this point the photographer dis-
appears for a period of ten minutes to prepare his
plate holder. When at last he announces the arrival of the fatal moment—"**all ready**"—you are
enjoying at least three kinds of nervous prostra-
tions and your happy smile looks like the tail end
of summer. Yet you wonder when you have sent
him one of these photos why the caricaturist fails
in portraying you just as you actually look in
your every-day life.

————:-:————

ALDERMAN EDDIE BEIN
Conducting the Famous Grotto Band Through Some Difficult
and Dangerous Passages.

Chemung river oyster fishermen are experiencing much trouble owing to the merciless onslaught of the carp upon their oyster beds. Jimmy Gilmore speared a carp in whose stomach he found one-half dozen of his finest breed Rockaways on the half-shell and two quarts of oyster spawn. The same has been reported to Charlie Woolf who will likewise mention it in his yearly report to the state fish commission.

Billy Hoffman has set his lobster pots for the spring run of the crawfish. The Chemung was so low last season that lobsters could scarcely ascend the rifts and Billy was obliged to get a shipment from Baltimore to supply his trade.

Frank Webb will cut his sandwiches a trifle on the bias this year, the square and panel shape cheese sandwiches being no longer fashionable. Bologna of course, will be served round as usual, between square slices of bread with ragged edges.

Elmira has a man by the name of Post who selects poles for the Elmira Water, Light and Railroad Company. I also know a Pole who selects posts for barb-wire fences. A strange coincidence, isn't it?

When it became known to the Indians that an army was approaching to shoot them into submission, they proceeded to arrange their war toilets. A committee was appointed to advertise for bids for the painting and decorating and in due time the contract was awarded to a firm composed of Alois Snyder and Lyme Fitch, two capable manipulators of the striping brush and to these gentlemen is due the entire credit for the weird and grotesque masterpieces upon the features of the red warriors..

Upon the arrival of Sullivan's army in the Chemung Valley, the "Indian club" was engaged in a Saturday afternoon eucher at Tax Miller's. Having no desire to mar the pleasant occasion by their untimely presence the Continentals betook themselves to Cronin's Lake St. Arbor where a spread of "Sauer-bradden" (a Dutch dish) was served while couriers were despatched to arrange a meeting with Red Jacket's warriors at the conclusion of their festivities.

TESTIMONIAL

O. K. Corn Salve Co.,

GENTLEMEN:—For several years past my corn has given me much uneasiness. Seeing your advertisement in our local paper this spring I decided to try a dozen boxes of your O. K. Corn Salve and began treating my corn according to directions on the package. I soaked it thoroughly for one hour in hot water and applied the salve upon it. For three nights I repeated the treatment as advised, after which I planted the corn in hills, and out of a half bushel of shelled "short ear" corn I raised ten acres of the finest quality "Long ear." Yes sir, I believe I have the finest looking cornfield in Chemung County and your O. K. Corn Salve did it. You may send me another dozen boxes at once.

Yours truly,

LIN GARDNER.

CHIEF ESPEY

The title of this picture is
"Oh Fireman Save My Child!"
Green lights and somber music.

SHERIFF DAY

On one of His Personally Conducted Tours to Auburn, N. Y.
My child, you are now in the iron clutches of the law;
therefore you must obey, else I shall cease to waste pet words
and resort to extreme harshness.

———:-:———

A farmer, who recently moved into our community has this
to say. He says, says he: That since moving into Chemung
county the milk from his old brindle cow rises to cream three
hours earlies than usual. That is not strange, however, when
certain mathematical conditions are taken into account. For
instance, according to the reckonings of our own thermostat
we find that the days in Chemung county are one and one-
eighth inches warmer and three inches longer than elsewhere,
thus the grass has that much the start of other localities and
the cow eats it that much earlier, therefore—but what's the
use going into details, the thing is a fact and that's all there
is to it.

That is not the only advantage we enjoy by living in Chemung county:. Again for instance. Its hospitality is un-
equalled. Everyone extends to you the glad hand at first

sight with its accompanied smile. It has an armory and military company to protect your business interests against foreign invasion. A river courses through its very heart, where you may bathe, fish or dump your ashes from your rear parlor window. It has also its doctors, though little need for them, and its undertakers are perfect pictures of despair, for were it not for their many side lines these gentlemen could not afford to remain in business.. Therefore do not hesitate, when you are looking for a new abode. All we ask of you is to settle with your creditors before you leave your present locality, because we don't like to have your sheriff take you from us after we have once taken an interest in you.

———:-:———

STATE SENATOR MURTAUGH.

In His Act of Reclaiming the Sullivan Monument.
So frail an article as this monument has proven to be, should not be left to the mercy of the elements, it should be brought at once (before any state appropriations are spent on

repairs) to the City of Elmira, and set up in one of its public parks then placed into the tender care and merciful hands of the "Hod Carriers, Bricklayers and Stone Masons unions."

MILES TROUT

Preparing Sullivan's Horses for Decapitation, as Described in an Article Which Forms Part of This Book.

The story of the discovery of many horses heads at the point where Horseheads is now located has been told so often that most of the readers are as familiar with the facts as the writer himself. But the absence of the balance of the horse has never been satisfactorily explained—at least, not until now, has ever a sensible solution to the problem been advanced.

Well, the truth of the matter is, that Sullivan's troops, on their way to the aforementioned suburb, were obliged to pass the blacksmith shop of

Miles Trout, (then the only horseshoeing studio in the Southern Tier. Miles had just patented a self-walking horseshoe and readily saw his opportunity to introduce it on a large scale. So he offered to reshod the footsore outfit at a much reduced price. The result was, that after depriving the horse of his head, the carcass, legs and the patent Trout shoe continued to meander into Schuyler County and, no doubt into Seneca Lake. I flatter myself therefore, at the knowledge that I am the first historian to probe this matter to such a depth, and feel that I am correct in my calculations.

SEYMOUR AND DOC.

Despise not these office shears my son, though they may be crippled and rusty and fit for the junk heap, for they are the making of some of our brightest newspaper men.

DISTRICT ATTORNEY BOGART

In a Case of the People

—vs—

Mr. and Mrs. Scrapp.

In justice to all the parties concerned in the case the artist has endeavored to describe the various exhibits in the possession of the District Attorney, viz:

—Exhibits—

A—Vile oath flung at head of Mrs. Scrapp by devoted husband on entering happy home.

B—Poker used by Mrs. Scrapp to ward off said vile oath.

C—Plaster cast of bridge of nose of Mr. Scrapp, which impeded further progress of said poker.

D—Set of false teeth worn by Mrs. Scrapp, show-
ing cavity formerly occupied by Exhibit E.

E—Wisdom tooth belonging to said cavity in
Exhibit D.

F—Implement used in removing aforesaid
tooth.

G—Abrasion left on said implement by contact
with aforementioned tooth.

H—Bottle containing sample of foul air in apartments of defendants.

I—Photo of Cop who attempted to arrest said Mr.
and Mrs. Scrapp.

COLONEL ARCHIE E. BAXTER

**A Through and Through American,
Upholding His Favorite Bird and Beloved Flag.**

TOMMY BARNES—Chef.

This man knows exactly how to tickle the palate at just the proper time.

————:-:————

ELMIRA AND STATE AFFAIRS.

For many generations our principal industry was the making of governors to fill approaching vacancies in the Albany Capitol.

The gubernatorial germ has so deteriorated, however, that the enterprise is practically on the slump. The last crop of aspirants proved a total failure which caused promoters to quit the game in disgust.

Once upon a time if a man was observed registering from Elmira at a New York hotel the word was immediately passed that the Governor was in the house. Elmira and governor were synonyms. Quite different now, though.

Every day one meets with evidence of motherly neglect by the awkward manner in which the American youth handles the pipe in his jaws. The boy child, to become a graceful and successful pipe fiend, should have his milk bottle taken from him at an early date and should be allowed to suck a pipe—the soft and delicate Meerschaum being preferable in accomplishing this end, as the cheap clay article is too hard and harsh on the tender gums. If mothers would exercise discretion in weaning their sons, it would be unnecessary in after years to send them to college to acquire the pipe habit. And at the age of ten or twelve they would have mastered the art to such an extent that any mother would have cause to feel proud of her offspring.

We show here a few samples of the untutored youth who was denied the pipe at that critical stage when he was beginning to look and act exactly like his pa, and when the milk bottle had filled its requirements. Surely no mother could willingly point her finger at such an array and exclaim with any sense of pride, "That is my son."

HIS HONOR THE MAYOR

Wondering if the City of Elmira will ever find someone to relieve him of his responsibilities so that he may return to his own dear, old Bargain Counter.

———:-:———

Fleas, though they be small creatures, possess wonderful power of the limbs. If man were built on an equal basis of strength in proportion to the flea, he would be as strong as an elephant, with the power to leap a half mile. In that case we should not require the underground passage at the Water Street crossing of the Erie railroad, for then we should simply jump the train and go about our business.

———◻———

The Lackawanna railroad recently had its appendix (which was located in the neighborhood of the Water Gap) removed and reduced the passage along its system some fifteen miles. This is considered a wonderful piece of railroad surgery inasmuch as it brings Elmira and New York fifteen miles nearer to each other without moving either city one inch from its original foundation.

FITCH CRANE

THE

Hustling Agent for the Maxwell Cars and Chase Trucks

The State Macadam road will shortly pass through Horseheads along this thoroughfare and right where my finger points stands my garage. I shall be pleased to attend to your machine troubles, load you up with gasoline and send you on your way rejoicing.

————:-:————

The "stuff" in this book was only intended to interest the people of Chemung county. If others have had the audacity to read it and it has afforded them any pleasure it serves them good and right and they need look for no sympathy from the author.

SOCIAL MENUS
Appropriate Combinations for Afternoon Gatherings.

AFTERNOON READINGS
Browning—and Lettuce Sandwiches
Toothpicks
Paper Napkins

———

QUILTING BEES
Mince Pie
Crullers and a Judicious amount
of Slightly Aged Cider

J. L. GREATSINGER

King of Rapid Transit.

Jake is a believer in speed of the motor but not of the body—or in developing the greatest energy with the least exertion.

HARRIS "THE LIVE ONE"

In His Peachy Orchard
Who believes that carefully selected and novel advertising
is the best means for producing large business crops.

———————

There are many ways to break a hen of her determination
to set (when she should be attending to more important duties,) but the simplest and most effective method is to smash
her nest with the flat side of a brick and clip her tail feathers with an axe, close up back of her ears.

Dear me, will our sensible women never cease to contradict
the rules of arithmetic by endeavoring to crowd a number
nine foot into a number four slipper?

"Say wife!   What on earth have you in that ice box that emits such an offensive odor?"

"Oh that's a quart of fresh Sauer Kraut the grocer just brought."

"Well, for land of goodness get it out of there as quick as you can and——warm it up for supper!!"

Coal dealers with an eye to business have also added wood and ice as a necessary adjunct.   Why don't our doctors follow suit and add to their sign: "Undertaking, Floral Designs and Tombstones"?

ASBESTOS.

PROFESSOR KRUG

Whose alluring strains between the acts have kept many a husband from deserting his wife to fill a ten minutes' appointment with the fellow next door.

ARCHITECT CONSIDINE

**Drawing up plans for the World's Fair in 1920 to be held in
Elmira, N. Y.**

———————:-:———————

When a man suddenly springs into prominence by some
daring act out of the ordinary, every nation in the world is
glad to pay homage and proclaim him its own flesh and blood.
The question of Peary's and Amundsen's nationality is now
settled beyond a doubt. Both of these gentlemen are
"Polelanders."

P. S.—Although this feeble joke is the original brainwork
of the Author, his situation is similar to Dr. Cooke's. It would
be difficult for him to prove it as there were no eye witnesses
on the spot when it entered his head.

O. C. WOOLF.

State Fish and Game Protector.

Mr. Woolf will gladly point out to you the difference between a spring sucker and a speckled trout. Should you hook
a trout out of season and wish to be enlightened on the subject, send for Woolf.

———————:-:———————

Elmira lies in the lap of a great sporting era, consequently
many expert hunters and anglers abide there. A game and
fish protective association is vested with power to hold annual banquets for the advancement of humane methods of
poking shot into partridge, quail and other game. Many of
its members are as yet unfamiliar with the plumage of the
aforesaid birds, as statistics of the Chemung County Farmers'
league show a decided falling off of their hen and turkey
crops in localities bordering a wilderness. Some of these
sportsmen are such skilled marksmen that farmers hasten
their cattle to shelter at the first discharge of gun powder.
This is no reflection upon the association, as it is not expected

that this efficient organization send tutors with every gunning
party to point out the real game bird from the domestic fowl,
whose plumage—to an excited hunter—look exactly alike.
But truly there should exist a law to compel such sportsmen
to pass a civil service examination before they be allowed to
drag a loaded gun through the woods by the muzzle.

———

Every good mother is more or less wrapped up in the future of her first born. What course the child will pursue is
with her an everlasting problem. One easy means of reading the kid's fortune is to give him a Bible and a deck of
cards. If he takes kindly to the Bible it is a pretty sure sign
that he'll be a preacher—if he takes to the cards, dollars to
doughnuts he won't be a preacher.

———

Captain REID and Musician WINNER

Lining up their Home Guard for spring inspection.

THE THREE GRACES OF THE ORIENT

HEAR NOTHING
SEE NOTHING, and
TELL NOTHING,
Are sadly reversed in our country.   Imagine our newspapers
existing under such circumstances.   We even disregard the
three cherished graces of our race:
HOPE
FAITH, and
CHARITY.
  Applied to our fashion of observation it reads:
HOPE—To do everybody.
FAITH—In nobody,
CHARITY—Unto your own body.

ELECTRICIAN GEORGIA
Illuminating the Neighborhood
  With apologies to Miss Liberty who has a similar job down
the way.

FREDERICK C. TOMLINSON

Of Casualty and Auto Insurance Fame

Fred says it is really a luxury to be bumped by an auto since his Insurance company assumes all the risks of your bodily injury. TRY IT.

———————————

While traveling aimlessly about the City of Elmira, you should carry conspicuously secreted somewhere about your person a copy of this book to use as your guide and bureau of general information. If you are biliously inclined or subject to spells of uncontrollable pessimism, you will find the presence of the book of decided benefit. It is the only article on the market today that will retain its face value after passing into the hands of the second hand book dealer, and like Aladdin's marvelous lamp, it is productive of many wonders. Perchance, if you are observed reading it, your observer may wonder what you are reading and why you weep so copiously and wonders where he might obtain a like book, that he also may weep copiously. Then again, as you enter one of our large and magnificent stores, its proprietor wonders how you happened to know that he was one of our advertisers, and wonders how he can part you from the contents of your fat wallet, and when he has done so to his satisfaction and you receive his "Au revoir" clutch, and "Come Again" smile, he wonders if he shall ever see your welcome face again.

Carry it with you by all means and when it is frayed and worn, purchase another one and do so some more.

J. S. VAN DUZER

Who handles the Elmira end of the Horseheads Creamery Co.'s Cream and Butter Trade.

"JONE" IS A LIVE WIRE ALL RIGHT.

A. S. FITZGERALD

The Penn Mutual Man

There are two ways in which you can easily recognize this gentleman. By a little, tiny, bald spot on the tip top of his head or his persistency in writing you up in the Penn Mutual.

I wish to make special mention here that ex-Sheriff Fitzgerald is a resident of Watkins, Schuyler County, where he spends his nights, but his days and income are consumed in Elmira. Like many others of the noted men in this book, "Fitz" lost his hair early in life and is somewhat sensitive over his misfortune. He therefore exacted a promise that the artist refrain from making this fact unnecessarily evident and requested him to place a hat upon the head which he did —as the reader will observe.

A celebrated patent medicine concern known as the "Seven Barks," recently brought suit against a sausage maker for copyright infringement in using the Trade Mark. The case was turned over to the Pure Food investigators which body found that the sausages were made of the following Seven Barks: Great Dane, Collie, Bull, Fox Terrier, Dach, King Charles and Yellow Cur, and was all that the name implied, thus returning a verdict in the butcher's favor.

BEN RECORD

Returning the customary salutation with the driver of the
Water Vehicle.

COUNTY TREASURER DEISTER

Guarding the Interests of the Taxpayers.

Please note that the left hand is thrust into the depths of
a receptable where it is fondling the half dollar which he has
laid aside for a copy of this book.

We seldom hear Sullivanville mentioned since
the county has sapped that locality of its best po-
litical timber, "But keep your hat on folkses!"
She'll corrode the rest of the county with envy
next August, in honor of her illustrious namesake.

GRANT DE VED

Proprietor Rathbun House.
The healthy and wellfed appearance of its landlord is a hotel's best testimonial.

What an ungrateful specie is the human race when we
look the situation over carefully. A set of vultures in human
form bent on doing everything (which is not a direct kin to
Adam) out of its due share of this world's good. We rob the
poor hen of her eggs because we can procure calico, laces
and feathers in exchange. Sometimes we are generous
enough to hand her back the empty shells that she might re-
plenish her system with sufficient lime to manufacture more
eggs. Yet we look that poor hen in the face day after day
with the utmost unconcern and, should she by a look or
sign intimate any dissatisfaction over such treatment, we simply wring her neck and serve her up amid gravy and dump-
lings.
    There is also "The Little Busy Bee" which some philan-
thropic poet has held up to the school child as an emblem of
industry and thrift. As soon as it has completed its season's

work and put its pork and 'taters in the cellar and closed its front door to the ravages of winter, some human fiend comes along with a pail and gathers in said winter's provisions and offers it in the market at 10c per card. No wonder the bees get their heads together and start on strike for they are keen to the injustice to which they are annually subjected, and no doubt, have formed a honey makers' union. This fact is borne out when they leave their factory in a swarm and locate in other quarters.—RURAL PHILOSOPHY.

The Quack doctor who advertised a special remedy for a certain disease spoke the truth when he said: "My medicine will straighten you out immediately."—And it did, as the undertaker will testify.

DAWDY

Whose "Staff of Life" has a state-wide reputation. It is especially adapted to camping purposes. Enclosed in paraffine paper and lays so light upon the system that it will float you in case you fall overboard.

POSTMASTER PRATT

An Intimate Acquaintance of Uncle Sam.

If ever there was a rank monopoly, the postage stamp business is it. There is no such thing as a baker's dozen. An extra one thrown in for good measure. In the stamp business one is compelled to buy of Uncle Sam and pay his price and he leaves you no room for profit should you feel disposed to resell his wares. Is that not a monopoly in restraint of trade of the worst sort?

At the baker's shop we get six for five cents or twelve for ten cents. At the grog shop by extending an invitation to a third party we get our drinks at the rate of three for a quarter, leaving us a profit of 5c on each round. Our street car companies offer a like inducement. Even our coal man will throw in a few extra skoopfuls of slate and screenings when we purchase more than one ton at a time. Not so with your "Uncle Dudley" who runs the stamp shop. You pay for every penny's worth, cash down or leave it.

Would it not look better and less piggish if occasionally a sign were displayed announcing a special bargain sale of shop worn stamps or remnants of some old prints? But no, this licensed monopolist palms off his old wares with the new and one only makes the discovery that he has been bamboozled when he applies his tongue to the tasteless stuff on the backs of the aforesaid stamps. If we are to lick our own stamps why not adopt the principles of the soda counter? Flavor the gum on your yellow stamps with lemon or vanilla, your read ones with raspberry, your brown ones with chocolate and your green ones with limes, then, if we must pay full price for them, we shall not feel so badly soaked.

I once knew a young fellow who was struggling to keep body and soul together by washing and pressing second-hand postage stamps and offering them to merchants at greatly reduced rates. These stamps were sanitary and palatable and in every way superior and much more desirable than those put out by the postoffice. Yet this energetic young man was hounded out of business and thrown into prison by the big Stamp Trust and not a word of protest was heard in the young chap's behalf.

Was Eve tempted by the dollar sign to devour the forbidden apple or was it a wise advertising dodge to attract the attention of the world at large?

EX-CHIEF JOE CAMPBELL

The Man Behind the Hose.
Joe was a fireman way back in the days before hose was invented and water was passed up the ladder by the dipperful.

The easiest way to get along in this world is to not let other people stick their noses into your business. And bear in mind, that this rule works both ways; also keep your own facial adornment unto yourself.

How many of Elmira's Sullivans can boast of
relationship with the lamented General? That is
the thing which is giving the genealogists much
concern. But what worries us most is how many
Sullivan Bros. and Sullivan Sisters are going to
offer special bargains during dedication week? So
that when we drive to town to attend the exercises
we shall be able to kill two stones with one bird.

BEN HALL

It's the man who writes your "Ads" that brings the business to your door. Ain't that so, Ben?

HADLOCK AND CLARK
Meat Marketmen.

The artist experienced much difficulty in producing a life-like picture of this energetic firm as the dog was very unruly and refused to remain quiet during the operation.

————:-:————

ALPHABETICAL KEY TO THE SITUATION.

A—Stands for "Alderman," elected by vote,

B—Is the "Bank" who discounts our note,

C—Stands for "Court House" the seat of Chemung

D—Is for "Drawbacks" of which we have none.

E—Stands for "Exempts" as everyone knows,

F—For the "Firemen" who handle the hose.

G—Stands for "Good thing" who gets the glad hand,

H—Is our "Hotels" the best in the land,

I—Stands for "Information" very cheerfully handed,

J—Is our "Jail" where the crooks are landed.

K—Stands for "Knowledge" dispensed at our schools,

L—Is for "Limbo" reserved for our fools.

M—Stands for "Monument" that was built with a rush,

N—Is for "New Roads", by Assemblyman Bush.

O—Stands for "Officeholder" who's sucking the plum,

P—Is "Prosperity", let the darn'd ole thing hum.

Q—Stands for "Queen City" the finest ever,

R—Is the stream they call Chemung "River,"

S—Stands for "Sheehan", the father of all,

T—Is the "Ticket" that gets in next fall.

U—Stands for "Umpire" who'll soon be shouting.

V—Is for "Visitors" here for an outing.

W—Stands for "Woodlands" so grand on our hills.

X—Is the "Ten Spot" on our currency bills.

Y—Stands for "Yours Truly," grasp it with a vim,

Z—Is that feller who signs himself   "ZIM."

LUNN AND HOLLOWELL

Thunderstorms carry no terror to the hearts of these
"Russelloiders."

CUSTARD AND KISTLER

Laundrymen.

Through whose business energy we are relieved of the "Yellow Peril."

Chemung County, in ridding herself in the Indian plague, adopted very much the same plan as the toper who decides to quit booze by tapering off gradually, lest the sudden shock should prove fatal to his enfeebled heart. Just so did Chemung County taper off from the genuine Indian to the wooden Cigar Store variety to lessen the shock which might come with the sudden release of that bad element and as soon as she could spare the wooden red man without endangering her entire organism she did so. Now we are absolutely Indianless.

Since the world began, religion has passed through many changes. Not so with Satan, he conducts his business in his same old way and seems to be prosperous as ever.

A traveling salesman who was detained by floods when informed of his mother-in-law's death wired home: "Go ahead with festivities; wash out; can't come."

CRONIN

The Arbor Man

Every day is Arbor day at Cronin's Lake Street Cafe and Restaurant.

T. E. LAFRANCE

The Carnation King

At whose greenhouses the wonderful beauties of nature
are developed by a master hand.

————:-:————

The Greek and Latin crammed into our school
children is perhaps a useless brain wrecking proposition. But the Hog Latin of early schooldays
was by no means an easy task to master. The
following is a sample verse in the Hog Latin
tongue, which every scholar was obliged to com-
mit to memory and recite by heart before it could

engage in the exercises during recess:
"One yaw, two Zaw,
Ziggazaw Zam,
Bobtail vinegar,
A tickelaw tam,
Harem, Scarum,
Sturgeon varum,
See, Saw, Buck.''
The whole meaning an equivalent of the numerals from one to fifteen.

BANDMASTER HAUVER

"Good morning men!"

If music hath charm to soothe the savage breast, then Mr. Hauver should have lived in Sullivan's time, when the Indians were having their celebrated uprisings. Surely with Hauver's melody we might have averted even the erection of the Sullivan monument.

JAMES FALSEY

President of the L. M. Association.

And Pilot of a fleet of native schooners that cross the bar daily, except Sundays.

———————— ■ ————————

To produce the first edition of this book it required four acres of solid trees for paper pulp, a half barrel of lamp black, five gallons of kerosene to mix with it; ten pounds of Honest Scrap smoking and five ditto for chewing; six packages Beeman's Pepsin Gum; half gallon machine oil; six months' credit with the grocer and the butcher; two note endorsers; 10 bushels of potatoes, many pads and pencils and every cussword in the profane vocabulary.

Will the genius with his inventive brain never quit his foolish capers? Here is a man who has invented a hen's nest that will fool the hen into laying twice a day. A description of the nest is given below and as no patents have yet been issued anyone desirous is at liberty to build them. The bottom of the nest is provided with a trap door which opens automatically when the egg leaves the hen and conceals the egg in a false bottom, and when the hen turns to look at the result of her day's labor, finds that nothing has happened, she is so ashamed that she immediately proceeds to lay another.

BILLY MAURER

"Der Grosse"

Compounder of Hassenpfeffer and many other appetizing dishes.

ROBT. BATTERSON

Merchant Tailor

"Bob" says that if ever woman gets her suffrage he'll be obliged to turn ladies' tailor. How could he do otherwise when she insists on wearing the pants?

————————:•:————————

DEDICATION OF THE MONUMENT

It is pretty nearly a certainty that in August 1912, Elmira shall witness the greatest military event since the rebellion. On this occasion the Sullivan monument will once more be dedicated and an armed and uniformed host shall again stamp down the fertile farms and rip up the rail fences of our struggling ancestors, to do honor to the memory of that great General, (Sullivan.)

Another item of equal interest to which we look forward

with much concern is the reopening of the old canal to admit seaworthy craft into the heart of Elmira by way of Seneca Lake and the possibility of fetching the nation's great battleships to our very hearthstone—to lend a formidable and fitting aspect to the occasion.

Captain Lewis Van Duzer of the Brooklyn Navy yard, who is soon to change his naval base to Horseheads, will no doubt extend us the courtesy of a few of his dry dock cruisers for that purpose with a detachment of able and experienced seamen to instruct us in the use of the big guns and the handling of the ships. The latter is a small item however, as we have many old case-hardened canalers left over who would volunteer their services to this worthy cause.

When the July sun is setting and the month of August is about to hatch, bear in mind to let those who lack experience drag their parched tongues in the seething summer dust, but you who attended the first dedication in A. D., 1879 (and suffered the tortures of the infernal regions) take heed and carry an ample supply beneath your belt and an emergency flask at the hip; for who knows that history may not repeat itself?

LINES TO THE MONEY MAD

Shoulder thy everlasting burden and hie thee to thy hapless mountain home and thy loveless family. There gloat over thy successes of today and, when thou hast glutted thine innerself with rarest indigestible viands and slept thy sleepless sleep, return again on the morrow and fetch back thy burden with thee.

M. DOYLE MARKS

President Elmira Automobile Club.
With an Automatic Piano-Player Accompaniment

The latest addition to a Fire Department (for localities where water mains freeze up and render the service useless) is an attachment to the fire engines which will roll up snow balls and shoot them into the flames by way of a nozzle. This will necessitate the storage of snow in back alleys and vacant lots and a competent gang of shovelers will be added to the service, The machine can be adjusted to any fire engine and bears the same relation to the engine as the "Doylemarx" piano player bears to the piano, except that snowballs will be released instead of delightful melody.

J. L CHURCHILL

The man who will erect the beautiful Baseball Monument
in Recreation Park to the Elmira Pennant winners in the fall
of 1912—IF!

Many changes have taken place since the beginning of this work, so that in some cases our story
and illustrations may not fit present conditions.
We ask the public to make allowance for the in-
tervention of time and join with us in offering
praise that none of our subjects have succumbed
to the inevitable, nor has even a single advertiser
kicked against our proposition and refused to pay.
This is what we call good luck, pure and simple.
We shall embody all of these facts in our closing
prayer, with special mention for the salvation of
those whose bills have not yet been rendered.

DEL GILBERT

His place is near the river. Drop in when you're down—
the water's (?) fine.

"Hash" is the Rich Man's Luxury and the Poor Man's Curse.
"As for me, give me liberty or give me death."

Regarding that famous dish, hash, I would
say the best way to make hash and the proper
time to eat it is as follows: To make hash, one
should use only meat and potatoes, a little chop-
ped parsley, an onion and pepper and salt. Many
cooks deem it necessary to add a bunch of cat
hairs and a few coal ashes—perhaps to aid the
work of the human gizzard, but as a hash cooker
I disagree with them on that point. That is drag-
ging a soup bone down to the lowest depths of
degredation. The soup bone cannot help its lowly
condition, though it was reared in the same en-

vironments as its close cousin, the juicy porterhouse. The same conditions exist in many large
families of human beings; where one son usually
develops into a rich gouty porterhouse and his less
fortunate brothers remain poor, worthless soup
bones.

Then, as to the proper time for munching said
hash: I should never select Monday for such;
Monday is recognized as the family wash day.
Hash and wash do not assimilate. Wash day is
bad enough but when your wife serves you hash
besides, it seems like flinging your poverty into
your very jaws and unless you are a gentle minded
man like myself, you will no doubt resent it, ev-
en though she is your beloved wife. Hash always
tastes better when one feels prosperous. That is
why millionaires smack their chops over the dish.

No. Sir! this is not a "Doylemarx" Piano Player. It is our
own patent hand maniputaling "Dogograph." The "Doylemarx" works entirely automatic and is easily operated by
anyone, but one must possess a delicate musical ear in order
to get the proper twist to the keys on this instrument.

Engagements for concerts and musicales now being booked.

Shall we believe the story of the golden harps of heaven, or are they simply gold plated?

TRY MY OWN
SWINGING COT BED.

MILLER

The Awning Man

A comfortable "Miller Swinging Cot Bed" beneath you and a handsome awning over you, while "Old Sol" is getting in his best licks, will give you a pretty fair idea of Paradise.

N. A. POWELL

Who Handles the Destinies of the Firm of
Gately & Co.

———:-:———

During the summer months, specially construct-
ed steel cars, highly disinfected will be run to and
from the Rendering plant on the Horseheads division. It has been discovered that much of the
precious odor concealed in the clothing of its employees has been allowed to escape in the regular
cars of late. The R. R. Co. realizing that its patrons were getting more than their tickets called
for, have taken steps to remedy this oversight.

HOWARD E. BAKER
Lumber Merchant

The lives of Lincoln and Baker were much alike in many respects. The former split the forest into rails and became president of the United States, the latter rips it up for high class building material and is the First Vice President of the Elmira Chamber of Commerce.

Two of our nation's greatest characters George and Carrie, both did it with their little hatchet. One cut down the cherry tree, the other cut up the juice.

We have many churches in Elmira and of almost
every denomination and for the benefit of those
whose time is not too much occupied for occasion-
al worship, we would say that they could do no
better than drop in and try our different brands of
religion. It will cost you nothing but the time.
We furnish everything for your comfort, the edifice, the soft cushioned pews, the music and prayer books and if your devotion is so profound that
you cannot keep awake throughout the service, a
sexton will provide you with a feather pillow.

BIG STAG MILLSPAUGH

Now Wearing the Official Antlers of the Elks
Lodge—''Hats off, Gentlemen!''

BILL HOMER

Managed to escape the camera. This portrait
was made from description by an able artist.

A WORD REGARDING OUR JAIL.

Not every community is fortunate enough to
own its own jail, nor is it always a fit place to
house a respectable law breaker. Elmira can boast
of a commodious detention resort. One may have
his choice of three distinct apartments, viz: The
unpretentious but sanitary whitewashed walls
with tobacco, pipes and refreshments; an uphol-

stered cell or the solitary dungeon, whichever
suits one's disposition and station. Its locks are
of the finest make which offer ample protection
against lynching parties and other social bodies
and under the trained eye of an armed keeper and
a hospitable sheriff one can feel perfectly at home
within its embrace. Therefore, if you are bent on
going to jail, kindly give us a trial and let us dem-
onstrate to you our efficiency in this respect.

FRED JENNINGS

The Produce Man.

Who keeps us in daily touch with Market
Quotations.

LEVALLEY AND McLEOD
The Well Known Plumbers, Steam Fitters and Furnace Men.

P. S.—Should we have another winter like that of 1912—Just leave it to us. We can turn your home into a veritable tropical garden, with but one artificial palm and our heating system.

————:-:————

"Many returns of the day," said the drayman as he dumped a cart load of unsold papers into the one million sworn circulation newspaper office window.

An Elmira teacher asked a freckled face pupil
for an essay on apples, and this is what he handed
her: "Apples is round, wid a stem in one end and
a worm hole in t'other. You kin buy dem in grocery stores and of Italian dagoes, but dey tastes
better when you steals 'em. De red ones makes
fine applesas and de green ones makes bad stum-
mick ache."

JOHN TIMOTHY SMITH
Our Democratic County Clerk.

Who is growing gray and beardless in the
faithful service of his party.

DR. KHARAS

When the Doctor was a mere child he bore every promise of becoming a handsome business man, but success in the Empire Mobile Car Sign business has changed him so that his own mother wouldn't recognize him.

P. S.—A man who has the advertising propensities so strong in him ought to get all that is coming to him and he surely got it when he bought that hat.

———:-:———

It is a well known fact that an Author's works become popular with his demise. Let us hope such is not the case with this work, as the Author has no such intentions at present, but sorely needs the money.

If you are run down and wish to be wound up and put in running order, write to "your own" Joe McCann of McCann's Tours, New York, to fix you up a health tour either by land or water. Joe's prescriptions are always beneficial and lasting.

THE LA FRANCE GARAGE TRIO

Here's a bunch of hustlers for you, and Pa, (the youngest of the party) has to take the back seat.

FRED FERRIS

Who Started Business with a Pair of Ponies, is
now Delivering Goods by the Car-Load.

———

A country justice who was about to swear a witness discovered that his Court Bible was nowhere
to be found. "Never mind, Your Honor," said the
witness, "I have in my pocket something that will
answer as well." Saying this, the witness held
aloof a large Swiss cheese sandwich, and uttered
these solemn words: "By all that's Good and
Holey I swear to the truth, the whole truth and
nothing but the truth."

Last year's temperance wave (in some of our neighboring villages) left the localities so dry that farmers were obliged to bore holes in the soil with an auger to plant their seeds and angle worms were bringing two shillings a dozen.

----◦----

"All the world's a stage," quoth Shakespeare. But that was before the discovery of electricity which made trolleys possible.

"TAX" MILLER'S.

Where you get the Base Ball news by innings, and other things too numerous to mention.

LAWYER HASSETT

A Busy Man.

Mr. Hassett deserves the Artist's special attention for his persistency in withholding his portrait till the eleventh hour and fifty-ninth minute of publication time. He's a good fellow so will let it go at that.

A kitchen girl who had charge of the pastry department in a wealthy household, objected to being called a servant, for the reason that the position she occupied entitled her to the higher title of "Dough-mestic."

PERSONIUS

"That's All"

Please note the tranquil expression of the photographer after requesting his victim (in the death chair) to remain silent for an hour and twenty minutes.

————:-:————

One doubtful clam will cast a gloom over the finest meal that was ever served.

————:-:————

The merchant who sits back of his stove and refuses to advertise his wares is nearly a thing of the past. He who waits for a customer to ask "Have you any so-and-so in stock?" is dropping out of prosperity's procession. The man who commands our patronage is the one who says "I have so-and-so to sell—come and look over my superb store and stock!" That is the man who draws the human flies to his commercial bee-hive and gains our respect.

Again I am impelled to speak in kindness of my martyred dog, "Patsy," to whose sweet and loving memory I so tenderly dedicated my Foolish History of Horseheads.

The dog so endeared himself to the members of Cashmere Grotto during the Horseheads Masonic Fair by proving himself a feature of the celebrated wheel. Said wheel which bears Patsy's portrait was later taken over by the said Grotto and is now part of its social work.

Alas! he wound up his short and checkered pants as honorably as ever a dog did, deserving of all the glory due his ilk. His mortal flesh, far too precious to mingle with the rank and file,

"NAY! NAY!!"

Far be it from such!

"Patsy" received a stately burial, shrouded in a potato sack with a solemn coon as pallbearer and sexton, his remains were consigned to their last rest on the banks of Newtown Creek, where dog angels may look down upon his silent tomb amid wild flowers, poison ivy and driftwood. Long live his memory, for he made many dollars for the Lodge while he lived. Yet he was but a dog.

F. N. DOUNCE

They say "King Coal" was a merry old soul,
But he didn't hold a candle to Dounce,
Who fills up our bin
With "Gilt Edge" to the brim,
Every ton weighs two thousand to an ounce.

The present year, 1912, is bound to be a banner year. A programme of State-wide and local interest is already laid out which promises to bring into our City many thousands of strangers who will come loaded with money to leave with merchants. This is the time to get busy. Advertise, and advertise in a way that will attract attention.

If our method of advertising suits you, then we invite you to come in on our Second Edition which will soon go to press.

AUTOBIOGRAPHY

With this volume I celebrate my fiftieth annual struggle with cruel fate. Yea, on the 25th day of May, in the Year of Our Lord, 1862, within the Canton of Basle, Switzerland, as the last rays of the golden sun were taking leave of the day and the cheese-makers were wending their "whey" homeward and the ice was "cicling" over the delicious Alps, a messenger, dispatched to a neighboring Inn (where, seated at a round table, absorbed in anxiety and pinochle) found my parent to whom he broke the glad tidings. The welcome manifested over my arrival was greater than I had anticipated, and richly repaid me for arriving so inopportunely. From that hour henceforth I have looked forward to this auspicious occasion, my 50th anniversary. On May 25th, 1912, I shall cross my half-century line, then farewell to my golden locks and welcome to those venerable gray hairs that are desperately struggling for supremacy.

The first half of my life was spent in lonely bachelorhood, the last half in blessed wedlock. One child, five dogs and seven cats have shared the joys and sorrows of our union, most of the latter having joined the life beyond. (Peace unto their ashes.)

My warmest regards to the land of my adoption, and to its people, for their kind and patient tolerance of my humble efforts. Those desirious of tendering their congratulations can do so by certified check, express or postal money orders; tokens of respect, marks of honor and rewards of merit in the form of tin and wooden ware will be gladly received by a maid in waiting at our kitchen door.

Yours with utmost sincerity,

THE PERPETRATOR

MR. BENNETT AND MR. GAYLORD,

Proprietors of the Enterprise Cut Glass Co.
The brilliancy of their cut glass would make the rarest diamond look dull.

This paragraph was set by our novelty Typist. I call him a novelty man because he can do a little of everything, as this paragraph shows. He can smoke, sing and shuffle his feet beneath the Lino-type machine without missing a word and when he gets particularly gay turns handsprings as he manipulates the keys and produces these marvel-velous results. When we engaged him, we did so at $7.50 per week, but truly, a man of his diversi-fied accomplishments is worth $8.00 of any firm's money. We are holding onto him purely out of charity, until he finds it convenient to leave us without compulsion. Any office desiring this wonderful article please address,

JIM DENT

REPORTER OFFICE

Horseheads   New York

CHAS. PULFORD

Member of the Well Known Construction Co.

Mr. Pulford is shown here meditating why Governor Dix could not as well have signed the Elmira dyke bill as to veto it.

Before closing, I must again allude to the pathetic and carefully prepared dying appeal of that noble warrior "Red Jacket," as he lay prone beneath the roughshod hoof of his conqueror, Gen. Sullivan: "General," said he; "Thy attitude is most annoying. I prithee remove thy hobnails

from my cedar chest for they tickle me much I as-
sure thee. May I also trouble thee for a light from
thy cigarette, ere we part forevermore?''

— ◦ —

LAWYER LATTIN

**Secretary of the Chemung County Agricultural
Society, Manager of the County Fair and
a Man of Many Other Activities.**

— ◦ —

Once a ''Rooter'' now a ''Fan,'' a cross between a human being and something worse. His
only aim in life is to make others feel miserable
by his wild wireless yelps which are intended to
spur his favorite team on to victory, but most always disturbs and confuses the players and lead

them down to defeat. We have no laws—either National, State or Local—to gag this individual and to kill him outright would be too humane, hence we must gnash our teeth and forebear until the end of time. Unfortunately every base ball city has at least a few of the aforesaid, who make life to the respectable baseball crank (the lover of fair play and equal respect for either team) a burden while the game lasts.

———————:-:———————

CALHOUN

Manager of Elmira's Base Ball Team.

Calhoun was the last man to get his face over the photographer's plate. He'll be the first, though when they reach for the pennant.

More special edition reprinted books from
New York History Review

*A Brief History of Chemung County, New York,
1779 -1905 with Index*

Harper's New York & Erie Railroad Guide Book of 1851

The Elmira Prison Camp

Our Own Book : A Victorian Guide To Life

NewYorkHistoryReview.com

www.ingramcontent.com/pod-product-compliance
Lightning Source LLC
Chambersburg PA
CBHW021336090426
42742CB00008B/624